Wicked World

Complex Challenges and Systems Innovation

Cover design and interior layout:
Jelle F. Post, Groningen

Illustration credits:
Lerone Pieters, Unsplash: p. 28
James Wainscoat, Unsplash: p. 51
Shutterstock: p. 96
Miguel Sousa, Unsplash: p. 148

0 / 20

© 2020 Noordhoff Uitgevers bv, Groningen/
Utrecht, the Netherlands

Any comments concerning this or other publications should be addressed to Noordhoff Uitgevers bv, Antwoordnummer 13, 9700 VB Groningen or via the contact form at www.mijnnoordhoff.nl.

ISBN 978-0-367-72353-8 (hbk)
ISBN 978-9-001-29696-4 (pbk)
ISBN 978-1-003-15449-5 (ebk)
NUR 801

The information contained in this publication is for general information purposes only. No rights or liability of the author(s), editor or publisher can be derived from this information.

WICKED WORLD

Complex Challenges and Systems Innovation

International Edition

Karel van Berkel
Anu Manickam

Noordhoff
Groningen/Utrecht

Table of content

Preface

We live in an era where almost everything is being transformed into something new. Everything is up for discussion. Power relationships are changing in many areas of our lives and in many places – no one knows whether we are moving in the right direction. Similarly, the downside of globalization has become starkly visible in recent times with climate change and the emergence of COVID-19. Our vulnerability has been exposed. We have been hit hard and we need to adapt fast – not only to issues related to our health, but also to how we organize ourselves in economic and social domains.

Since the beginning of our collaborations, our partnership has been repeatedly challenged by complex issues. We share a passion for (almost) insoluble problems and have been on a journey that has brought us to appreciate the need for systems approaches when addressing personal, organizational and social challenges. Our focus on exploring 'problems behind the problem' has resulted in a deeper understanding of systems dynamics.

This book is about complex problems that do not respond to conventional approaches. We share our insights and the resulting sensemaking framework for systems innovations in *wicked worlds*.

We would like to thank everyone who has crossed our paths in the past thirty years: clients, teams and individuals we have worked with, our students from Master programmes who investigated complex problems using this approach and helped validate its emergence over the years. Their examples, questions and collaborative thinking made this book on complexity and systems innovations possible.

In particular, we wish to thank our publisher Petra Prescher for her confidence and support in realizing our book, which aims to make complex systems sciences accessible to current and future professionals in policy and organizational management and support them in dealing with the unprecedented challenges of a Wicked World. In addition, we thank Ada Bolhuis and Manimohan Manickam for their help in realizing a well-edited book. To Ans Assies from Hanze University we are grateful for catapulting the international edition into print earlier than planned. We also would like to thank reviewers and readers of our Dutch edition for their acknowledgements and validation of the book's impact on their work.

Most importantly, we would like to express our thanks to our families for their enthusiastic and continued support. They have been a source of immense inspiration for us.

Anu Manickam and Karel van Berkel
June 2020

Introduction

S imple or complex? We prefer life to be simple and ideally, we like to avoid complex issues. When there is no way around such issues, we break them down into smaller, more manageable parts, we look for unambiguous causes that can be eliminated and seek simple solutions.

This compulsion to simplify complex challenges, *wicked problems* as they are also referred to, is ineffective when confronting them. In a complex world, change does not unfold smoothly, according to our needs, calculations and plans. Then, there are also coincidences and crises shaping developments.

Current approaches to problem-solving and traditional methods of facilitating change will only take us so far. No magic formula exists to prevent an economic or health crisis, cope with the flow of migrants or combat global warming. In fact, despite all the progress we have made, we find ourselves caught in an irrevocably tangled web of interrelated problems that we try to solve through simplification.

The only way for us to bring such *wicked problems* to heel is to accept their complexity and acknowledge that there are no easy solutions. *Wicked problems* call for a different approach. Systems and complexity theories provide insights to understand and unravel complex and dynamic *wicked problems*.

Taking a systemic view yields new possibilities for interventions. It offers a new paradigm for policy, strategic action, change, planning, organizing, leadership and cooperation. Systemic interventions are applicable to persistent challenges facing individuals, families, teams, organizations, networks, countries, but also, other living systems.

Systems innovation gives us tools to more effectively handle complex issues. Understanding and dealing with divided and vested interests, mapping developments and connecting the dots, changing the playing field, simplifying rules of the game, are glimpses of this approach.

This book puts forward a coherent and systemic approach to problems in a Wicked World. It offers practical examples to convey this new way of thinking and to begin applying it in organizations or policymaking.

By openly embracing the complicated and intractable nature of complex problems, we can better understand why things happen the way they do and create new solutions.

1

Wicked world

How do we view our world? There are three dominant lenses. The first is one of 'control' in which we assume that everything can be planned. The second is what we call the 'bubble world'. In this worldview, opinions and biases are dominant and group-driven. The third is the 'complex' world where we accept the paradoxical, unpredictable and dynamic nature of things due to interconnectedness.

Three worldviews

The worldview of a person determines how they look at problems and what actions they take to achieve their desired results. The three worldviews therefore impact assumptions, behaviours and results of the respective groups embracing them.

The controllable world

We can, to a certain extent, succeed in making our world manageable, familiar and reliable. We have achieved this through planning, calculating, experimenting, replicating, learning and designing. We can plan certain aspects of our lives: we can pave roads and build bridges, heat our homes and cure many diseases. Facts, laws, routines, rules of thumb, evidence of effectiveness, habits and regulations help us to lead our lives without undue confusion. When a problem arises or something happens to thwart our plans, we diligently search for a quick solution. We have faith in specialists and their methods. For a moment, our world seems manageable once more. At least until something else happens.

The manageable world is only one part of our reality. Many problems that seem manageable in the short term may prove to be more complex in the long term 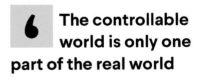 **The controllable world is only one part of the real world** or when seen in a broader context. Fossil fuels were once considered an outstanding resource for heating, mobility and industrial use until we realized that the Earth was warming-up and climate change was becoming a *wicked problem*.

Brexit, United Kingdom's withdrawal from the European Union, was an appealing and obvious decision for many (in the UK) and it seemed a manageable option. This changed as problems emerged. These included negotiations on the scope and duration of a transition, the financial obligations and risks to both the UK and Europe, post Brexit EU and UK citizens' rights, challenges of a border between the Republic of Ireland and Northern Ireland, expectations and disappointments regarding a new trade deal with the EU, common challenges and shared resources such as military and policing agreements, anti-terrorism, space and education programmes and human trafficking.

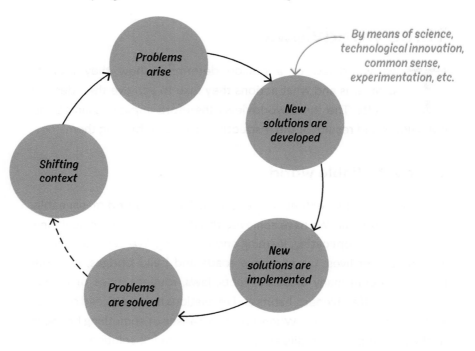

The examples show that often actions we take may have unforeseen consequences, thus resulting in new problems. We are not always in control.

The bubble world

For many in the Western world, life has become less predictable and less safe. We worry about our incomes as robots and automation increasingly replace jobs. Some worry about our prosperity and the economy as newly developed countries are catching up and may overtake us. Will we be able to master our fears of cybercrime and terrorism?

A study by Shepherd and Kay (2012) shows that people tend to avoid societal issues they find too difficult. This effect is heightened when the issue at hand is serious and urgent. The inclination is to defend the status quo rather than pursue information and embrace change.

In her book *Political Tribes* (2018), Amy Chua describes how groups who feel threatened often retreat into ethnic or cultural tribalism. They isolate themselves, close ranks, begin to think in terms of 'us and them'. They feel they are being attacked, bullied and discriminated and often react defensively. Chua explains how capitalist market-based thinking has led to a growing divide between a small, wealthy elite and the rest of the population. Individuals demand what is rightfully theirs based on their tribal standing. Another phenomenon of *political tribes* is that new tribes are emerging. An example of this is the growing diversity in sexuality and self-identification, represented by the acronym LGBTQQIP2SAA (lesbian, gay, bisexual, transgender, queer, questioning, intersex, pansexual, two-spirited, asexual, allies). Amy Chua explains that similar tribal circles are emerging in many places around the world.

A new development, in an effort to cope with uncertainties, is the large number of people seeking support from digital networks.[1] They look for support from like-minded individuals and use social media to develop and reinforce their opinions, behaviour and identity. This results in homogeneous 'bubbles' in which Twitter and other social media is used to (re)interpret facts[2] and check opinions with others who share similar beliefs. These groups or *bubbles* may be scattered all over the world, but they share similar opinions, fears and anxieties. These developments have seen politicians and corporations cashing in to serve their interests whilst individuals in these *bubbles* also profit from visibility and popularity.

Bubble worlds are sensitive to populism, manipulation and fake news as 'popular' views are spread via websites and social media (Bruce, 2017). Big data technologies and personal profiling enhance the impact of widespread views and altered news. Often used in politics, this trend is called 'post-truth-politics'.[3] Political framing, conveying a message through words and imagery to appeal to a certain group, is a way of simplifying reality.
Professor of Public Administration Hans de Bruijn distinguishes between frames that resemble a project and those that resemble drama. A project frame is exploited by those who want to 'project' authority. They do this by asserting their version of a problem, its causes and often simplified

solutions (De Bruijn, 2016). This simplification makes a complex reality more manageable: 'When the sea level rises, we need to build higher dykes.' In contrast, a drama frame, focusses on the players instead of the core issue. There are villains, heroes and victims in a drama. The drama frame plays on emotions: 'Immigrants are thieving opportunists who cause trouble for normal citizens, which is why we should send them back.'

Web-algorithms fuel the *bubble world* by social profiling. This helps political and commercial parties to bring specific information to specific target groups. This is known as micro-targeting. Your 'click behaviour', location, spending patterns, friends and search history are used to ensure that you land in a specific information *bubble* and this means that you are less exposed to deviating facts and opinions. By *living in bubbles*, our perspectives and biases are confirmed (Pariser, 2011).

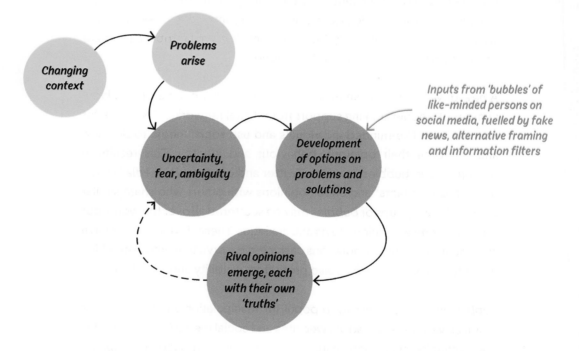

Inputs from 'bubbles' of like-minded persons on social media, fuelled by fake news, alternative framing and information filters

People feel comfortable in their *bubble worlds* as their view of the world and opinions are reinforced and thus begin to feel less threatened. The trend towards *bubbles* promotes self-opinionated and opposing views that results in antagonism against those who have dissimilar outlooks: rich versus poor, urban versus rural, young versus old, women versus men, and so on. Such behaviours entail grave risks. These *bubbles* resemble what Janis describes as 'groupthink',[4] which leads to collective rationalisation of behaviour, stereotyping of others and often enforced conformity. When we conform, there is no longer any fact-checking or comparing points of view with someone whose ideology differs from our own (Van den Bos, 2017).

The European Commission is conscious of these risks paired with the increasingly polarizing effect of *bubble worlds*. A panel of experts were asked to provide recommendations to

'In a complex world, like-minded individuals seek support in their *bubbles*

combat disinformation. Their report recommended a code of conduct for those responsible for hosting or distributing information on the Internet. This would apply to online platforms, news media and fact-checking organizations. While ensuring room for freedom of expression, transparency and clarity of views need to be safeguarded. The report also recommends investing in media literacy of citizens, cybersecurity and quality of journalism (European Union, 2018).

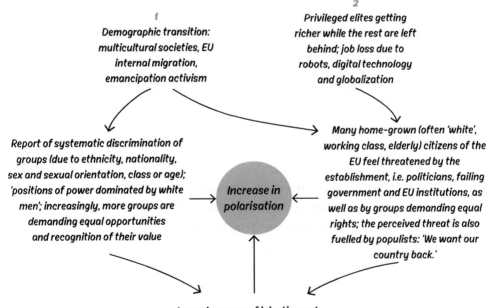

1
Demographic transition: multicultural societies, EU internal migration, emancipation activism

2
Privileged elites getting richer while the rest are left behind; job loss due to robots, digital technology and globalization

Report of systematic discrimination of groups (due to ethnicity, nationality, sex and sexual orientation, class or age); 'positions of power dominated by white men'; increasingly, more groups are demanding equal opportunities and recognition of their value

Increase in polarisation

Many home-grown (often 'white', working class, elderly) citizens of the EU feel threatened by the establishment, i.e. politicians, failing government and EU institutions, as well as by groups demanding equal rights; the perceived threat is also fuelled by populists: 'We want our country back.'

A growing sense of injustice and dissatisfaction
Fundamental principles become subject of discussions:
- *voting rights for all*
- *government serving all*
- *equality in education, work, etc.*
- *responsible citizenship*
- *respecting differences*
- *assumed solidarity*

The complex world

The world we live in has become complex, characterized as being VUCA: volatile, uncertain, complex and ambiguous. The waves of crises that have daunted us in recent times bear witness to this: the financial crisis of 2008 coupled with the Euro-crisis; Brexit in 2019 and currently the COVID-19 pandemic of 2020. Each crisis uncovers deeply rooted weakness and structural deficiencies. It confronts us with our inability to be in control.

Wicked problems

Horst Rittel and Melvin Webber (1973) recognized that not all problems are the same. Simple problems can be easily defined and divided into manageable parts, which can then be solved. For more complicated problems, professionals or experts may be needed but these can still be solved. They referred to these types of problems as *tame problems*. Examples of *tame problems* are fixing a bicycle, kidney transplants and sending a rocket to the moon.

Wicked problems defy simple solutions The second type of problems identified by Rittel and Webber often prove to be more elusive and defy simple solutions and these are referred to as *wicked problems*. Part of what makes them complex is that different stakeholders define the problem differently, each with their own perceptions of what is important and what needs to be done. Simplifying these problems often make them worse.

Wicked problems are problems:
- that can be defined in more than one way;
- that cannot be broken down into smaller problems;
- that involve multiple parties and multiple interests;
- that invoke different solutions from different parties;
- that trigger a new problem for every solution;
- that develop in unpredictable ways.

Wicked problems defy a simple explanation. We can illustrate this with the case of natural gas extraction in Groningen, the Netherlands. Gas extraction was embraced as a reliable, long-term solution for its energy supply. This euphoria was intact up to 1986 when the first earthquake in the region took place. Since that time, more than one thousand tremors followed and were tolerated. However, the turning point came in 2012 with an earthquake that caused visible and significant damage. Gas extraction was a major contributor to the treasury and the lobby of the NAM, the oil and gas company, was substantial. However, Dutch politicians and NAM, could not ignore protests and the hazards of gas extraction for the inhabitants.

Technical solutions were initially proposed to appease inhabitants and service victims but these were inadequate due to the nature of what was at play. These included different needs, differences in *sense of urgency*, bureaucracy, power differences, social and cultural costs next to economic costs, significance of gas in facilitating energy transition, concerns about energy supply and affordability, fears regarding health and safety, which in turn led to increased distrust, social unrest, inadequate communication, new coalitions, etc. The rest of the country was sympathetic but also wary of the money flowing away from them.

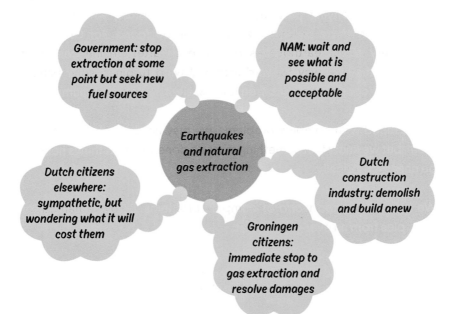

Wicked problems are interconnected with other key challenges. Gas extraction is linked to energy transition, which is related directly to climate change. This makes the problem of gas not only an economic but also an environmental issue. The earthquakes not only resulted in material damage but also caused emotional and psychological impacts.

We know that *wicked problems* are framed differently by different stakeholders with very different solutions. In the illustration, we see how the government, NAM, residents in the area, citizens elsewhere and the construction industry responded.

We also know that solutions for a *wicked problem* often creates new problems or aggravates existing ones. When the government ordered drilling to be stopped at Loppersum, where extensive damage had taken place, the earthquakes increased further south. Halting gas extraction also meant that long-term gas contracts needed to be revised at additional costs. This meant a double loss of revenue. Also, alternative energy supplies meant additional costs for all as home-grown gas was cheaper.

Finally, *wicked problems* are unpredictable. It was unclear what the end game of 'no gas' from Groningen fields would bring and how to resolve the many problems connected to it. But as is often the case with *wicked problems*, underlying patterns become more visible, which provide guidance for where potential solutions can be found. For Groningen, uncertainty about earthquakes remain even after drilling ceases. It was clear that the way forward included wind turbines, solar panels, sustainable construction, gas-free homes, electric cars, heat pumps, etc.

When faced with complex problems, we may not know how to tackle them, but we know that something must be done, and that things need to be changed radically.

We live in a *wicked world* of complex problems. Below, a handful of examples from an ever-growing list:

Influx of refugees and reactions from host populations	Urban migration and depopulation of rural areas	Shifting geopolitical relationships with new global powers
Role of Internet and social media	Energy transition	Threat of terrorism
Impact of Uber, Airbnb and online platforms	Financial/economic crises and recoveries	Plastics in our oceans

Loss of jobs and robotization	Virus pandemics	Outbreaks of livestock disease
Greying society	Regional development	Drug-related crime
Trump's America	Internet of Things	The future of Europe
Obesity	Genetic modification	Influx of asylum-seekers

Super wicked problems

There is another category of problems that are even more complex, the *super wicked problems,* which for example, capture the essence of global warming (Levin et al., 2012). *Super wicked problems* have a larger and more pervasive scope and *sense of urgency* about them. The most recent example is that of COVID-19, although the jury is still out on whether it is a *wicked* or *super wicked problem.*

Super wicked problems are defined by four characteristics:
- Time is running out.
- Solutions are offered by those responsible for the problem.
- No central authority has legitimacy to solve the problem.
- Problem-solving is postponed with irrational assumptions about the future.

Climate change illustrates features of a *super wicked problem.* The *sense of urgency* before global catastrophe strikes is captured by the 'minutes to midnight' metaphor. Many professionals are convinced of the need for action to mitigate climate change but rampant disagreements abound on how much time, and how to attack the issues. The clock ticks as discussions continue, increasing risks and urgency.

We all contribute to global warming. Even as we take small steps in the name of climate change, we continue to exacerbate global warming through our behaviour and daily habits – how we eat, drink and travel. Similarly, politicians will endure the use of fossil fuels even when promoting renewable energy.

Climate change does not have a single authority that calls the shots. Current power houses are divided: some deny the problem, Trump being an example; others, developing countries in particular, demand the burden be borne by wealthier nations even as they push for greater economic and social prosperity; and there are others who wait, convinced that only a concerted effort will help. These responses also reflect our tendency to ignore the present and assume, or hope, that it will work out in the future.

The misplaced assumption by politicians and policymakers dealing with immediate goals and short-term solutions to appease the electorate when dealing with urgent problems often comes at a high price. It may be too late but often, as in the case of climate change, youth and citizens take to the streets to challenge authorities who do not respond adequately.

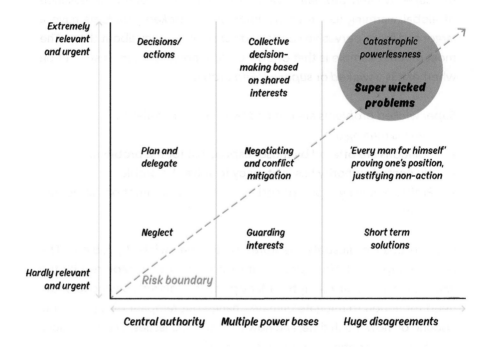

The illustration reflects how we react to problems and where the dividing line is that could lead us towards risks and catastrophe. The onus is on us to recognize *super wicked problems* and the need for timely response.

Context determines the approach

David Snowden and Mary Boone (2007) designed the *Cynefin framework*, which distinguishes four different contexts of decision-making: simple, complicated, complex and chaotic problems.

Simple problems are stable and display clear relationships between cause and effect. If we are in traffic and the light turns red, we know what is happening and how to react. If the situation is clear to us, the solution is usually within our reach. *Best practices* are usually available to solve simple problems.

Complicated problems are more intricate and often best left to experts. We may recognize that there is a problem, but multiple solutions may be possible, which is why we need experts to investigate and choose appropriate solutions. Complicated problems include sending a rocket to the moon, which requires extremely precise calculations and protocols. Each component needs to be tested and perfectly assembled. In the process, experts learn continuously and develop blueprints for improving such processes. *Good practices* are often available for solving complicated problems.

As far as **complex problems** are concerned, there are no 'right' answers: the context is intricate and continuously

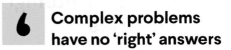

Complex problems have no 'right' answers

changing. The future is difficult to predict and decisions or solutions usually affect other related aspects. Developments in the European Union are a good example of this. Every decision at every political level, both within Europe and beyond, causes the context to change entirely. With Brexit, decisions of the British people have impacted not only internal affairs such as the borders on the Irish island for example, but has in fact dampened the demand to leave the EU by some groups in other EU nations. Managers also deal with complex situations in which forecasts and proposed decisions can become irrelevant before implementation. For example, a major client decides to take their business elsewhere, or a competitor has an innovative new product, or that COVID-19 strikes. Strategies are instantly outdated. In a *wicked world*, the context is constantly changing and managers can no longer assume that decisions with help from experts will guarantee that everything will work out. When faced with complex problems, they 'wing it' and see what happens. If the action was successful, they continue on the same path, if not, they choose another course of action. There is no way to know how effective an action will be until after it has been taken.

In a **chaotic context**, there is no time to explore and investigate, action is needed. When a fire breaks out, you have to act immediately: seek safety and get help. Practice and preparing for fires may help to act spontaneously but each fire is a different story and there is no time for analysis, action is the only requirement. Only after the facts, can you explore what happened and think of how to prevent and deal with such problems in the future.

It is important to differentiate between simple, complicated, complex and chaotic problems, to know which problems can be managed and how to deal with them. Simple and complicated problems are served by prevailing approaches that offer tools for efficient and effective solutions. In contrast, complex problems need new approaches. A growing number of studies based on complexity sciences offer directions and tools for the new class of complex problems.

Systems intelligence and complexity theories

How can systems thinking help us understand *wicked problems*? Which factors allow *wicked problems* to thrive? Various systems and complexity theories provide answers to these questions.

Systems and systems thinking

A system is an independent whole with its own unique boundaries and identity, made up networks of relationships of various elements. Systems can be physical: a car, a human being, a brain, a virus, a computer, a region, etc. They can also be organizational or conceptual: a business, a sector, a network, a professional group, an accounting system, a political or economic system, country, etc.

Incidents are part of larger systems

Systems thinking has proliferated since the 1940s (Merali & Allen, 2011). Whilst enormous progress had been achieved through analytical reduction and specializations, the scientific community recognized that narrow scopes of investigations meant that connections outside of the scope of study were lost. In the meantime, systems thinking has increasingly gained momentum. Systems thinking ensures that attention is given to interactions both within and across systems. Problems and solutions always take place in the context of interactions:

when there is an argument between two people in a team, there needs to be a team solution; when a team wins a match in football, it is never only the few that scored a goal but it is the success of how the entire team played.

We need to understand that different approaches are prevalent within systems studies. Many systems thinking approaches assume that you can have control and plan. On the contrary, complexity-based approaches are founded on the premise that new developments emerge from interactions, regardless of intentions and goals: evolution instead of planning and design.

Systems approach based on assumption of control	Dynamic systems approach
Systems exist independent of their environment.	Systems are connected to their context and other systems are part of it.
Systems consist of components (sub-systems) which are in turn made up of other components.	Systems consist of interacting systems that influence each other's developments.
Complex phenomena can be tackled by breaking them down into smaller problems.	Complex phenomena are tackled by understanding relationships between problems.
Systems naturally seek equilibrium.	Systems can be thrown off balance through escalations and may even cause new and unexpected directions of development.
Systems in a given category resemble one another: best practices are applicable.	Every system is unique with its own history and context: best practices will not work.
A system's past, present and future are distinct features.	A system's past can have adverse or positive impacts on its present and future.
A system can be adjusted independently of other systems.	Change in one system changes the context and landscape of other systems.
System behaviour is knowable, plannable and manageable.	There is no certainty in system behaviour in terms of knowing, planning and controlling it.
Interventions are separate and specific for each system level. Effects of intervention are localized.	Any intervention affects all levels as micro-macro relationships are found everywhere.
Change is achieved through rational and planned efforts: analysis, action, evaluations. Mistakes are to be avoided.	Change is achieved through trial and error, learning from mistakes and coincidences. Outcomes are uncertain due to systems dynamics.

Systems approach based on assumption of control	Dynamic systems approach
Change is achieved through consensus.	Change is achieved by creating room for diversity.
Strategic planning to realize strategic change: vision for the future is critical.	Strategic change involves responding promptly to changing contexts: focussing on *the next step* is critical.
Systems are managed in a hierarchy. Effective change is implemented through top-down decision-making and a plan of action.	Dynamic systems are self-regulating and self-organizing. Change can be triggered from all directions, inside and outside, and are never linear. Sudden or gradual possibilities may emerge.

Complex adaptive systems

Complex Adaptive Systems (CAS) theory is a dynamic systems approach, in which complexity is leading. The theory assumes disorder, the unexpected and coincidences. It appreciates that problems may exert unintended influence on one or more systems in unpredictable ways. It also emphasizes the significance of local context and the subjective realities of stakeholders. CAS also highlights that change is continuous and creates new circumstances in which no one has the power of control or decision-making. In analyzing problems whilst bearing in mind these qualities of complex systems, new insights and perspectives offer suggestions for change.

CAS, like other complexity theories, has its own vocabulary that differs from conventional change management. These terms offer a different lens. Examples are: *systems dynamics, adaptation, simple rules, patterns, attractors, emergence, agents, weak signals and self-organization.* We explore this new language to demonstrate how *wicked problems* can be analysed systematically in the rest of the book.

John Holland (1992) introduced Complex Adaptive Systems theory. He described how systems change and reorganize themselves internally in response to problems arising in their environments. Key characteristics of complex adaptive systems[5] are:
- Relations, interactions and feedback mechanisms are present within and between systems.
- Agents in systems are semi-autonomous; interacting with each other; constantly adapting, learning and evolving with changes.

- Evolution implies seeking strategies to fit changing landscapes.
- With complex problems, there is no central control mechanism, instead self-organization emerges.
- Local interactions collectively generate macro-level systems changes (new qualities, interactions, patterns, etc.) that bring about new order to complex situations
- Co-evolution across systems ensues due to interactions with other systems.
- Minor variations in initial conditions can lead to immensely different outcomes.
- Complex adaptive systems function best when order is combined with some chaos, also known as *the edge of chaos*.

Tackling wicked problems in practice

The theoretical principles of CAS require interpretation to make it workable to address practical challenges of *wicked problems*. These working principles have been incorporated into our *systems innovation framework* that is explained in the following chapters.

These working principles include:
- Map details of the problem including the context.
- Adapt responses to fit the continuously shifting context with alertness to its unique features.
- Expect unpredictability, escalations and lack of control.
- Collaborate with others across disciplines; communicate a lot but listen attentively.
- Explore a variety of perspectives – visions, approaches, solutions, etc.
- Engage stakeholders, 'agents' in complexity terms,[6] in the process.
- Understand stakeholders' paradigms and communication norms to improve effective intervention possibilities.
- Identify shared values and common interests.
- Identify potential coherence in the complex challenge through visualizations.
- Look for *leverage points* – small interventions with large effects.
- Look for potential side effects of each selected approach.
- Learn and adapt continuously – experiment, use trial and error to learn

Systems dynamics

Wicked problems arise within and between systems. Systems, sub-systems and relationships between systems can be drawn to show interconnections.

To illustrate, in the Netherlands, three distinct 'regional' systems can be identified, these being, the main metropolitan centre (Randstad), other major cities and rural areas. Systems dynamics between these systems show emergence of new patterns such as urban migration, increased prosperity, attractiveness, traffic congestions, crowding and rural degeneration.

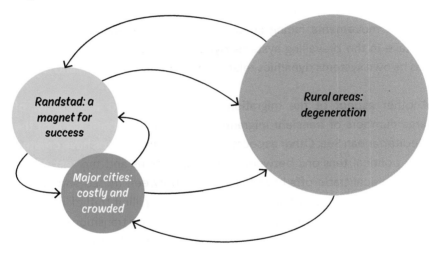

The 'Randstad' is a motor of economic growth in the Netherlands.[7] [8] Growth is not as strong in other parts of the country and smaller municipalities, especially in peripheral regions, are lagging behind and becoming less attractive to young people.[9]

Differences between the Randstad, other main cities and rural areas are creating developmental patterns that are difficult to understand without understanding interconnected system patterns. Rural areas are facing issues, such as economic and demographic decline, ageing populations, unemployment, lack of infrastructure, that are affecting quality of life and future prospects. The Randstad also has its share of issues such as congestion, negative effects of mass tourism, inflated housing market and labour market shortages. Similarly, larger cities close to rural areas have become centres serving rural communities with essential and recreational facilities such as hospitals, schools, stores, sports and cultural facilities, but also for work and to commute to other parts of the country. This Dutch example is typical of urban-rural systems dynamics elsewhere in the world. On a different scale, similar systems dynamics are evident with the magnetic pull of Western countries (prosperity and success) draining lagging economies (depressed economy and prospects) of its wealthy and youthful populations.

An example of this is, increasing waves of illegal migration to Europe across the Mediterranean Sea impacting both European and African countries. It is important to acknowledge that refugees rightfully seek protection and shelter and need to be supported in their flight from conflict. This sub-system of migrants seeking asylum are part of the larger migrant movements facing European and Mediterranean regions and partake in the prevailing systems dynamics. This sub-system however has its own systems dynamics related to its specific situation and issues.

Another aspect of the migration context relates to the impact of large numbers of transient migrants on countries on both sides of the Mediterranean Sea. Other aspects include: refugee camps have created new political tensions between bordering nations and the rest of EU; new political trade-offs have taken place between the EU and Turkey to 'manage' the surge of illegal refugees; growing illicit trafficking trade, detention of migrants in poor facilities and prisons in transition countries like Libya; increased feelings of anxieties and growth of nationalism in segments of EU population, regional and national politics, in part due to economic recession, job-loss, loss of national homogeneity and 'threats' to national identity; perceived and increasing powers of EU, etc.

To deal with *wicked problems*, a first important step is to map related systems and sub-systems to make dilemmas, paradoxes and interconnections visible.

Systems diagrams

Capturing what the 'story' is, is a useful way to grasp complex challenges. *Systems drawings* help visualize relationships between events, experiences, people, interests, themes and so forth. We have included numerous systems diagrams throughout the book to illustrate how these 'narratives' offer insights into what is happening.

Systems diagrams serve as a narrative account of how different aspects relate to one another, including connecting past, present and future. Different stake- 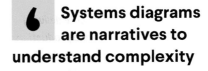 **Systems diagrams are narratives to understand complexity** holders have different drawings about the complex problem based on their perspective. When stakeholders compare and discuss their different versions, a new collective diagram emerges. We illustrate how this works through the case of company Medioc.

Medioc, a production firm, was facing disappointing results and members of management had different ideas about what was going wrong. They each singled out one aspect as the main cause with a single issue as the problem. These simplifying cause-effect narratives were supported by facts and figures to explain what went wrong: production numbers, financial results, absence of the floor manager, number of customer complaints, clocked overtime in the given period, etc. However, there was agreement that the business was heading in the wrong direction.

To get a better grasp of how the different problems were connected from a systems perspective, they created systems diagrams for each of the issues raised. Each diagram tells a story about that issue.

The drawing on their 'ad hoc' practice captures how they solved their problems as they arose to keep clients satisfied. The 'repair' process became normal, clients accepted this even if they were not completely happy and thus structural changes were pushed away.

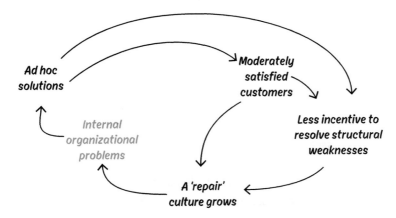

In another story, the members showed how problems were connected and contributing to other problems.

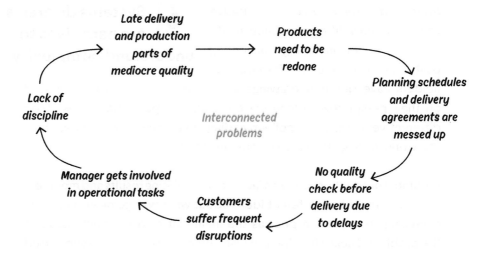

Both stories also show opportunities for addressing problems. When the members got together and compared their stories, they realized that both drawings were 'right'. They continued to discuss the issues at length and identified key aspects that needed to be addressed: problems being interconnected, ad hoc solutions, general malaise in corporate culture, excuses being the norm, attacking structural weaknesses and customer satisfaction. They then created a new diagram to connect these aspects.

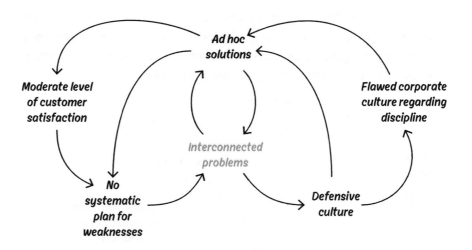

This drawing brought their stories to a single narrative, which then allowed them to explore possible interventions together. The strategy for change was endorsed by the whole management team and captured as *systems drawings* to connect all key aspects to improve business culture and 'up their game'.

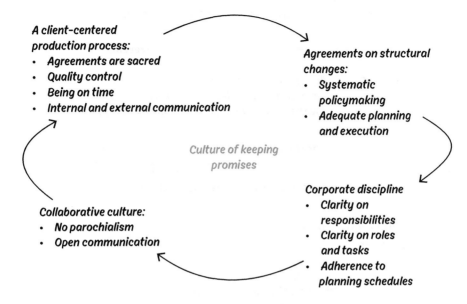

A client-centered production process:
- Agreements are sacred
- Quality control
- Being on time
- Internal and external communication

Agreements on structural changes:
- Systematic policymaking
- Adequate planning and execution

Culture of keeping promises

Collaborative culture:
- No parochialism
- Open communication

Corporate discipline
- Clarity on responsibilities
- Clarity on roles and tasks
- Adherence to planning schedules

The company had come to terms with what was wrong and have confidence that business results would improve if staff collaborated, had more discipline, listened to customer needs and promises were kept. There was a better appreciation for clarity on roles and responsibilities and a focus on long term structural changes. Drawing their stories and working on uncovering their personal narratives was an important first step for them.

Change

In a complex, dynamic and unpredictable world, things work out differently than we planned or hoped. Controlled, step-by-step approaches to change are not effective in a *wicked world*. We see repeatedly that carefully calculated blue-prints are overtaken by unforeseen circumstances making such plans redundant. At other times, interventions have unintended side effects or aggravates the situation, which then instigates huge resistance.

Traditional approach

We have indicated how traditional change models tend to focus on linear or causal change processes aimed at improvements and innovation. A widely used example is Kurt Lewin's three-phase change model (1947).

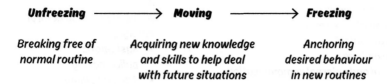

Unfreezing ⟶ *Moving* ⟶ *Freezing*

Breaking free of normal routine	*Acquiring new knowledge and skills to help deal with future situations*	*Anchoring desired behaviour in new routines*

Linear intervention models fail to account for chaos, complexity, the unexpected or the element of chance. The main focus is manageability, with little attention paid to differing interests and power of stakeholders.

Linear intervention models may take the form of a circle, but the process remains linear.

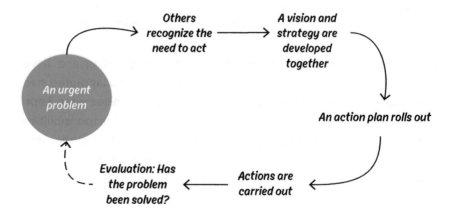

Changing differently

In seeking new intervention models for complex challenges, the following considerations need to be taken into account.

Complicated versus complex problems

We already described differences between complicated and complex problems. Complicated problems can be solved by specialists using scientific analysis and calculated steps. Complex problems, on the other hand, are connected with other problems and arise from dynamic interactions of stakeholders and systems. Such problems cannot be solved by specialists alone.

The 2018 UN Climate Change Conference in Katowice was the United Nations' twenty-fourth attempt to reach effective agreements on climate change. The UN wants all parties to be heard - resolutions paved by compromise and watered-down solutions. Complex problems are not solved by gradual steps focussed on gaining consensus.

Micro and macro impacts

Local incidents always impact local contexts, but may also have unexpected impacts elsewhere, often creating changes on a macro level.

To illustrate, the nuclear disaster at Fukushima devasted local communities but also saw massive shifts elsewhere: nuclear energy plants were shut-down, a global awareness and reconsideration of nuclear energy followed, with a new impulse for other energy solutions, consumers and governments alike.

Another example, the Twin Towers incident on 11 September 2001 and the subsequent response of the United States resulting in worldwide polarizations, demonstrates micro -macro level consequences.

Economic and political crises

Economic and political crises can have similar impacts. Due to an unexpected economic crisis in the United States in 2007, the housing market stagnated, leading to the collapse of two American banks, which in turn, escalated the economic crisis in the US. This in turn, triggered a major global credit crisis and a deep political crisis in Europe.

It is important to understand that interventions addressing local issues may trigger escalations in other systems levels.

Mass movements

Mass movements and mass communications frame developments and need to be considered when designing intervention models.

The escalation of refugee and migrant numbers entering Europe have caused unexpected consequences and responses at the local, national, regional and European levels.

Social media were hugely responsible for the growth of the *gilets jaunes* (yellow vest) protests in France. It began in November 2018 as a protest against rising fuel taxes on petrol and diesel but soon expanded into a protest against rising costs across France. Similar protests spread to other countries.

A 'hashtag' (#MeToo) launched in October of 2017 went viral on Twitter to explode into the #MeToo movement against sexual harassment and assault of women globally. This movement, fed by social media, brought about dramatic changes in organizations and individual's lives.

Management executives seem to be caught off guard by self-organized mass movements. It is important to understand that mass communication through media supports bottom-up initiatives and movements.

Local conditions

Change models must take into account local conditions. Each system, each context is unique. *Best practices*, the recipe for success for a given situation, cannot simply be copied into a different context. When change takes place in systems, history and geography play an important role.

Interpretations of reality

Reality is in no way objective or unambiguous. There is no such thing as 'the reality'. Interpretations of reality reflect viewpoints of specific persons or groups. In complex problems, various stakeholders are involved and could include scientists, religious groups, trade unions, shareholders, environmental activists, politicians, etc. Each group has its own worldview and interpretation of reality. This means that complex problems are defined differently by different stakeholders.

Perceptions of all stakeholders need to be considered when designing interventions. Also, how stakeholders relate to each other also determines if solutions are imminent. Coalitions are needed for solving complex problems and could include creating power coalitions. However, when escalations arise, outcomes are unpredictable.

Disruptive innovations

Disruptive innovations are a rude awakening for *business as usual* and make plans for change irrelevant. Personal computers, smartphones, artificial intelligence, robotization, self-driving cars, genetic engineering, 3-D printing are examples. Often, such developments are under the radar of organizations.

Being alert to developments outside one's boundaries, is obligatory for leaders of change in a *wicked world*.

Interactions

New insights, patterns, phenomena and organizational structures can come out of interactions spontaneously. Tensions between the Muslim world and the West, the Euro crisis, rise of nationalism in Europe, effects of social media and youth climate change protests are some examples. Interactions between top-down and bottom-up initiatives also contribute to change whereby self-organization processes are reinforced.

Different system levels

Spontaneous or prompted changes impact different system levels. An intervention at one system level – a business, a province, a country, a profession – will affect other system levels as well. Organizations do not typically give much thought to what their corporate strategies mean for the lives of individual employees or the broader environment. Businesses have long assumed that their core activities, profit maximization and being a good employer were their primary goals. They did not feel responsible for the environment or depletion of natural resources. Likewise, for a long time, individuals did not realize that their lifestyles, air travel, car ownership, food and energy consumption, etc., were impacting Earth's macrosystems.

When Maureen and Tony Wheeler wrote their first *Lonely Planet* travel guide in 1973 to encourage individual travel, they did not envisage that mass tourism would create havoc for many cities and communities. An article in a Dutch newspaper describes the *Lonely Planet* guides as the largest gentrification machine of the travel sector: 'Everywhere you go, the same thing happens in poor neighbourhoods of major cities: yuppies arrive, the locality becomes hip and former residents are effectively priced out of the area' (Bouma, 2018).

Two operating systems

To 'change differently', revisions are needed to existing organizational structures and processes. In a 2012 article published in the *Harvard Business Review*, John P. Kotter states that today's organizations must have two complementary operating systems in place: one to take care of matters that can be planned and managed, and one to deal with rapid and complex changes.

The first operating system focuses on achieving effective and efficient operating processes and optimal results. This operating system includes monitoring and managing structures and supportive instruments such as hierarchical structures and functions, departments, planning, budgeting, specialized staff, data inputs and analyses. A change trajectory involves *business cases* and special project teams that will support and guide change from A to B. The trajectory will be monitored through the process for adequate progress. This operating system works for simple or complicated problems.

Build flexibility through dual operating systems

Dealing with complex problems in their dynamic and increasingly changing contexts demand a different operating system. One that can respond quickly, flexibly and creatively. Kotter (2018) identifies eight accelerators that need to be simultaneously and continuously part of this second operating system. The most significant difference between this and the traditional operating system is that the process is guided through a coalition formed by networks of 'volunteers' from across the organization.

Characteristics of operating systems for effective change (based on Kotter, 2012 & 2018)

Operating systems	Change	Characteristics	Process management	Measuring
'Business as usual'	Developing business cases	Traditional management system: hierarchy, departments, positions, planning, budgeting, experts, staff, procedures, instruments, incentives, evaluations, accountability checks Bureaucratic and political interests	Change goals Project team Road map or plan	Baseline, interim and end measurement

Operating systems	Change	Characteristics	Process management	Measuring
Rapidly changing complex contexts	Networking	'Volunteer army' from across the organization Dynamic and political interests	Process guided by means of eight accelerators aimed at 'big opportunities': 1 Creating urgency 2 Establishing a company-wide guidance team 3 Establishing strategic vision and initiatives 4 Promoting voluntary participation ('volunteer army') 5 Removing barriers to promote action 6 Celebrating relevant quick wins 7 Maintaining urgency and focus 8 Integrate successful methods into organizational structure	Seek, act, learn and adapt immediately

In conclusion

As human beings, we have the ability to discover relationships and patterns and to predict how things will unfold. However, we live in a *wicked world* where chance, disagreements, unforeseen power and external influences can cause subtle changes and power struggles where outcomes are uncertain. The complex world can never be fully understood or planned as everything is constantly evolving and interconnected. We struggle with the *wicked world* as it relentlessly escapes our grasp.

Systems and complexity theories can help us deal with complexities of the world. These theories show how *wicked problems* emerge in a landscape of systems constantly reacting to each other. Uncovering underlying systems dynamics will make *systems innovation* possible.

2

Systems analysis

Every system develops an identity which determines how that system is positioned in relation to other systems. A system must develop a *sensitivity* to change. Systems that are relatively insensitive to changes around them will lag behind and ultimately will become outdated. Systems maintain themselves by their ability to respond adequately to changes. When a system changes, it influences its environment, its relations and the nature of such relations change. New themes, new forms of collaborations and new routines emerge.

Systems analysis framework

We are constantly confronted with *wicked problems* in the news: new epidemic outbreaks, human trafficking, geo-political developments, drug abuse, endangered species, affordable and accessible health, safety of whistle-blowers, malicious computer hacks, sexual abuse, etc. This list is a small sample of issues we need to address. Ideas and solutions are rife but time and time again we have seen how difficult it is to find ways to resolve complex challenges.

Systems analysis is the first step in realizing *systems innovation*. Awareness of feedback mechanisms, vested interests, communication patterns and power relationships are indispensable for system innovation.

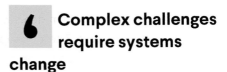

Complex challenges require systems change

The model for systems analysis establishes the foundation for a change method we call *systems innovation*. It builds on Complex Adaptive Systems theory and the systems dynamics framework of Manickam's Cluster Emergence Model[10] (2018).

The systems analysis framework incorporates four characteristics: identity, *sensitivity*, *responsivity* and *connectivity*.

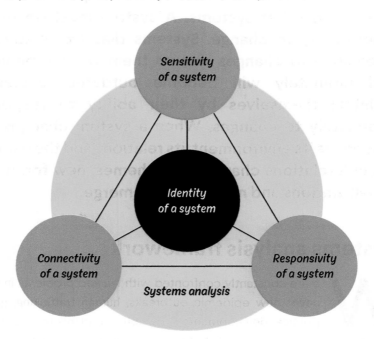

Identity

I dentity of a system deals with how a system sees itself but also how others view it. The concept of *identity* is used in connection with individuals, groups (teams, family, friends), organizations (businesses, social institutions), networks (economic clusters, LinkedIn connections) or communities (regions, countries). Systems can be physical (buildings, computer networks), organizational (senior citizens' lobby, agricultural cooperatives) or conceptual (feminism, culture). Systems also have purpose and goals they want to achieve (Ackoff & Emery, 2017).

A system's identity is not fixed. It can evolve with time, and with changing features. Villages surrounding urban centres are often engulfed by urban sprawl and lose their identity when they are integrated into the city's legislature. Cities too can change with time: Singapore was initially a simple fishing village. It became a harbour thanks to British trade negotiations, they also brought migrants from China and India, making it a multicultural society. In more recent times, it has evolved into a modern city state, often identified as 'best practice' for its many achievements.

All systems, be it a person, city or region, have multiple, overlapping identities. Perspectives, motives, interests and context, for example, frame how a system is perceived. 'Identities are socially constructed and highly complex.'[11] A person could be a parent, sister, engineer, volunteer, amateur musician, band member and philanthropist and depending on the situation, purpose or interest, one or more identities is prevalent. Similarly, a region could also have different identities. For example: Northern Groningen of the Netherlands as a lagging region with high unemployment; the largest European gas reserve; an important heritage site for its unique natural and cultural landscapes; an earthquake-zone; a gateway to North Sea energy for European hinterland, rural, etc.

 Systems have multiple identities

More aspects of systems' identity: it has defined boundaries – it is clear who (or what) belongs and who does not; there is a past and a future; and there are routines and rules. It is also important to understand that systems interact with their environments – they mutually influence each other; and that systems are in systems. To illustrate: a person lives in a neighbourhood in a village, which is in a province, which is in a country, is part of a continent on Earth, which, is part of the universe.

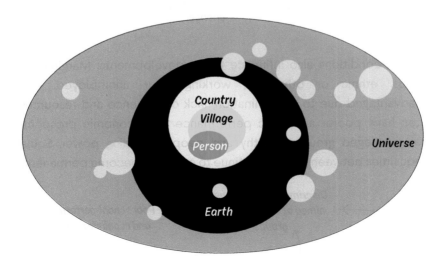

Changes in a systems' identity is dependent on its:
- history and contextual factors;
- stakeholders and their perceptions;
- patterns and routines;

- implicit and explicit rules governing interactions between stakeholders.

These factors offer both risks and opportunities for *systems innovation* and need to be part of systems analyses. We will explore these factors.

History and environmental factors

The development of a system's identity is influenced by factors including history, geography and culture. This is known as *path dependency.* Contexts of a system dictate actions and the resulting outcomes, and hence shape its future. Changes push the system's context in a specific direction, which in turn, affects subsequent actions. For instance, a small football club can grow more easily into a large football organization than becoming a large accountancy firm. The history of the system shapes its developments. Similarly, if other football clubs in the area have more fans, money and better players, it will be difficult for that club to reach the Champions League.

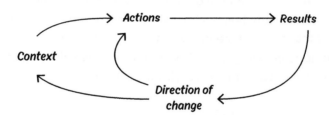

Cultural conditions also influence future developments. Marginalized groups, ethnic or otherwise, working poor, unemployed, etc., disadvantaged due to discrimination, lack of influence and resources, often have poorer academic performance and economic prospects than privileged groups, wealthy and people wielding power. Social inequalities between groups continue to grow and become permanent.

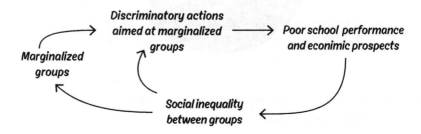

Path dependencies have inherent systemic risks (Manickam, 2018). Another type of *path dependent* risk is 'limits to success' (Kim, 1992), also known as the *Icarus paradox*. Icarus is a figure from Greek mythology who attempted to escape from an island by creating wings using beeswax. He was so successful in his flight that he flew too high and too close to the sun. The beeswax melted and he plummeted into the sea.

The *Icarus paradox* is often seen in sports: when teams become successful, they stick to their winning strategy and become complacent. They disregard the competition who has since improved their play (the environment), and wind up in a downward spiral of losing matches. This 'limits to success' pitfall can also be seen in cities that have been successful in promoting tourism. They painfully discover how mass tourism impacts their residents, who pay the price, including loss of 'their' city.

We often see that consistent and tremendous effort in a chosen strategy yields exceptional results. However, there are limits and when this is

> **The history and context of a system influences its identity**

reached, a downturn or negative effect is seen: using painkillers to allow you to perform when in pain can bring exceptional results, but there is a limit which, if exceeded, will cause dependencies or cause illness, and therefore negative capabilities. Similarly, your great product may be exceptional till your competition has innovations that overtake your market share. Collectively, as businesses race to excel and flood markets with products, the market becomes saturated or resources are depleted.

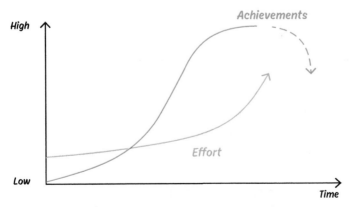

Adapted from: Daniel Kim, *Systems Archetypes 1* (1992)

Another risk of path dependency is the *lock-in effect* . When huge vested interests are dominant, choices outside of such interests is very difficult. Where extensive gas infrastructure and expertise are present, it is hard to develop strategies for energy transition outside of gas (Balanyá & Sabido, 2017). This also applies to digital gadgets and software. It is hard to switch to a different operating system once you are used to it: Apple, Android, Microsoft have *path dependent* risks once you are initiated into their systems.

System change takes place in times of crisis and innovation

Path dependency affects everyone and every system, with inherent risks but also opportunities. Systems primarily change in times of crisis and radical innovation. There are intersections for changing directions, also called *windows of opportunity* (Sull & Wang, 2005). These intersections could be starting points of *path creation* (opposite of *path dependency*). The Fukushima nuclear disaster prompted a turning point in energy policies for many countries. Our identity takes a leap at significant crossroads of crises and major events like graduation, marriage, job loss, death of loved ones, etc.

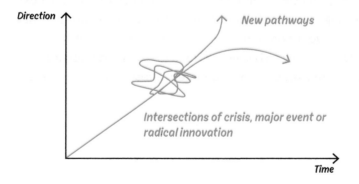

Daniel Kim (1992) describes a different scenario: '*success to the successful*'. This scenario comes into effect when a business is successful. Successful companies have easy access to credit and talent: banks are eager to lend money to successful businesses, and everyone wants to work there. Where higher calibre staff are hired, quality of the organization improves, and this makes the company more attractive to investors, and it then attracts better staff. Often, this success is at the expense of other businesses.

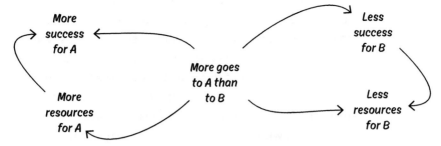

Adapted from: Daniel Kim, *Systems Archetypes 1* (1992)

A related effect of systems interacting with each other is that changes (innovations) in one system trigger changes in other systems: Uber and Airbnb have changed both business and consumer boundaries and identities.

Path dependency and *path creation* trigger systems change and *systems innovation*. Both crises and successes need to bring about transformations since systems need to continuously renew their identity or become out-dated.

Stakeholders and perceptions

A system's identity and its development are shaped partly by its stakeholders. A child (as a system) develops its identity under the influence of its parents, siblings and relatives in the initial years. The influence of these stakeholders changes as different stakeholders play different roles in their development. School and teachers become strong influencers when the child starts school; later classmates and friends may exert a bigger influence on their development; and this continues, with new stakeholders replacing or exerting new influences.

Stakeholders may exert opposing influences on the development of (system) identity due to their differing views and perceptions on what is 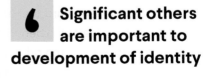 **Significant others are important to development of identity** important. A good example of this can be traced to the organizational structure of companies which proliferates conflicts due to opposing goals and incentives. This translates to each department pushing for their interests: sales department demands flexibility to meet customer needs; quality assurance department wants uniformity and process control; whilst management focusses on bottom-line, profits and deadlines. It helps when companies have strong shared focus, vision, purpose and commitments: *'Selling as many quality products as possible while minimizing costs'* but this needs to be at the forefront and not forgotten. When disruptions occur and the core mission forgotten, opposing interests and distorted communications may take over at the cost of the business as a whole. Conflicting groups vary in their power and influence on the system. In the healthcare sector, it is possible for *'bed occupancy'* to become more important than delivering *'quality patient care'* or the focus on *'treatments'*.

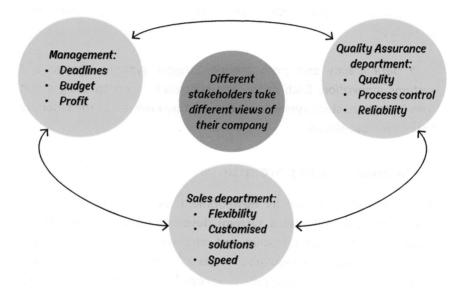

Stakeholders also have different roles in systems developments. Some stakeholders act as guardians of the 'established order' (*status quo*). Judges and the police force are stakeholders in society who have been appointed to safeguard the 'established order'. However, in the face of change, individuals who benefit from the *status quo,* exert their influence to resist change. On the other hand, stakeholders who may benefit from such changes are eager to topple existing structures and paradigms. Booking.com, Netflix, WhatsApp, Uber, Ryan Air are all examples of disruptions to how society and businesses were organized. There is a conflict of interests between traditional businesses and the newcomers in these sectors, who are trying to influence the direction of change.

However, other stakeholders, such as the general public, residents, consumers and investors are sometimes 'invisible' within a system, despite their ability to exert a great deal of influence. 'Hidden' stakeholders can be important forces to contend with.

Developing patterns and routines

People constantly interact with their immediate environment, which results in interaction patterns and routines, which then translates to *culture* when they apply to larger groups of people. Culture determines what is right and shapes our behaviour. Patterns and routines offer many advantages in day-to-day life. When driving a car, all our actions and responses are automatic: accelerating or braking at traffic lights are routines. Routines and patterns make us predictable and help others know what to expect in interactions. Often, roles emerge during interactions.

Defined roles have both positive and negative effects on innovation and renewal. When roles are traditionally defined and static, relationships of dependency emerge: between men and women, teachers and pupils, leaders and followers, bosses and subordinates. Assigned roles can sometimes foster undesired patterns: violence, intimidation, etc. (Lünnemann et al., 2010).

> **Identity: other people know what to expect from you**

Habitual patterns and routines reduce alertness. Weick and Sutcliffe (2007) show that organizations that have strong control cultures due to the nature of their business, are especially prone to risk due to the strict protocols. The efficiency of control systems in these organizations result in staff not prepared for unexpected incidents. In airlines, nuclear power plants and the emergency wards in hospitals and clinics, people become inattentive to minor changes and deviations from 'the norm'. Patterns and routines can slowly slip into disarray when no checks are in place.[12] This can be a gradual and insidious process in which targets and standards are constantly lowered. New situations call for new behaviour, yet fixed patterns and routines impede such efforts. They tend to prolong existing behaviour even when it has ceased to be effective.

Systems are challenged to adjust their behaviour, standards and values and assigned roles when new stakeholders bring their own sets of patterns and routines and when other systems introduce new technology. We see this in China's new-found economic and political influence on the global stage, Donald Trump's approach to the us Presidency, the #MeToo movement, the upsurge of e-commerce and social media, the advance of mobile technologies and 3-D printing and the introduction of robots in healthcare.

Attention to the development of patterns and routines, both positive and negative, is vital. In dealing with negative patterns, we are better off attacking them as they arise whilst long-standing patterns of behaviour are hard to crack. A long-term smoker is more difficult to influence than someone who just lit their first cigarette. Positive patterns can be reinforced by creating circumstances in which new behaviour is supported, encouraged, rewarded and safeguarded. The identity of a system can be nurtured in this way to increase its chances of survival.

Implicit and explicit rules

Every system has rules that help maintain that system. Ideally, everyone in a given system will follow its rules. When stakeholders no longer comply with the rules, the identity of that system will change. Donald Sull and Kathleen Eisenhardt (2015) took the idea of *simple rules* for developing a systems identity in complex environments and operationalized it. There are two types of rules: 'how to take **better decisions**' and 'how to do **things better**'. It is important to limit the number of rules: three to seven rules are ideal.

Rules for better decision-making	
Rules that establish boundaries	• When we want to innovate, we collaborate with at least five of our clients. • We always work in interdisciplinary teams.
Priority rules	• We consider quality more important than price.
Rules for stopping what you are doing or had decided to do	• In a Casino, play 100 games or until your money runs out.

Rules that describe 'how something should be done'	• Listen carefully to what others say; let them finish before responding. • Use your time productively. • Learn from previous processes and results.
Coordination rules	• Everyone must participate. • Decide where you can effectively contribute and then act accordingly.
Rules on timing	• Buy tech stocks when performance is low (late summer till December) and sell when high (January into early summer). • If you have trouble sleeping: Avoid going to bed before 11:30 pm; do not read or watch TV in bed; get up at the same time every morning.

In complex systems, simple rules guide behaviour. Using computational modelling, Craig Reynolds (1987) discovered how simple rules could explain bird behaviour when they flock together as swarms. He discovered how birds in flocks focussed on those closest to them and have three rules: avoid collisions, fly in the same direction as those closest to you and stay with the flock.

Principles governing complex systems also apply to human systems. Complex systems are not managed top-down or through detailed instructions, but by interacting players in the system who individually comply with simple rules.

In the armed forces, a high priority is placed on simple rules and swarm-based strategies. This is true not only of 'swarming' drones, but also  **In complex systems, simple rules guide behaviour** for operations in conflict zones far from headquarters where the local conditions and local intelligence are decisive for where, when and for what purpose the various units are deployed. This can succeed only when units continue to communicate with one another. The introduction of simple rules and swarm-based strategies has drastically changed the identity of the army in combat situations: local interaction and self-organization have replaced top-down command structures.

Another example of simple rules can be demonstrated in youth football. Parents are deeply vested stakeholders in this system. They are often emotionally involved in the game and shout instructions from the side-lines. This has led to an increasing number of incidents on and off the playing field, affecting the youth negatively. To tackle this problem, countries like Germany and the Netherlands have introduced simple rules: there is no referee, children decide for themselves; stakeholders (parents and other supporters) are at least 15 to 20 metres away from the pitch; coaches from both sides supervise the match together and stand side-by-side by the pitch.

Sensitivity

N ext to *identity*, an effective systems analysis requires exploring the degree of *sensitivity* of the system in question. Having a good 'radar' system that provides timely alerts on deviations, new developments and threats on internal and external matters is critical. This allows actions to be taken and if needed, to reinforce the system.

When investigating a system's *sensitivity*, four aspects need to be heeded:

- complex systems dynamics;
- drivers of change;
- weak signals;
- sensitivity to attractors.

Complex systems dynamics

Recognition of complex systems dynamics does not happen by itself. When obstacles arise, we tend to rush to resolve the issue instead of exploring how such obstacles may be related to other issues. Yet, it is more important to respond to underlying systemic problems rather than only tackle the obstacle that surfaced. We can compare this to taking medicines to suppress a fever instead of figuring out what is causing the fever.

In February 2018, the Dutch Police Union presented a report in which they warned about the risk of the Netherlands becoming a 'narco-state'.[13] Their report highlights how petty criminals had built up assets in the last twenty years and have been able to infiltrate the housing market, travel agencies and the retail sector and have become a force to be reckoned with. They were targeting prominent members of the society, such as mayors, aldermen and journalists. with threats and extortions. These developments reflect an alarming number of signals of a 'narco-state'.

The use of the term 'narco-state' generated many reactions on traditional and social media. A major Dutch paper, NRC *Handelsblad,* published an article that summed up the issues that were connected to the report and the subsequent responses (Meeus & Schravesande, 2018):

- growth of the drug trade;
- policy of tolerance related to drugs;
- limited capacity of the Public Prosecutor's Office;
- organized crime activities: cannabis cultivation and production of synthetic drugs;
- presence of mafia dealings in cocaine in Amsterdam;
- criminal infiltration of a fishing community to transport drugs in open seas;
- drug transport through container ships;
- involvement of motorcycle gangs;

- the Netherlands as a logistics hub for Western Europe;
- money laundering through the real estate sector;
- drug-related crimes leading to 'liquidations' in Amsterdam;
- priority to combating 'drugs' resulted in less resources for combating firearms trade, which caused heavy firearms to enter the market, leading to increased gun violence.

The list is not just a summary of facts and incidents. These related and interconnected issues interact to display complex systems dynamics. No one issue stands on its own; no one person or party can untangle the 'mess'; no one person can determine the way forward or discern which intervention is best. At the core of *wicked problems* lies the adage '*solving one problem creates a new problem elsewhere*'.

Complex *systems dynamics* is often evident in systems that have been pushed to extremes. One good example of this is the state of affairs surrounding global food chains. Where local farmers and local neighbourhood shops were commonplace, serving local customers, modernization has taken food production out of the 'local' to mass production and global scales in many countries. The dominance of global food producers, supermarket chains, monopoly of seed producers, pesticides and other agricultural suppliers, pervasive global value chains with corresponding long-haul logistics are components of the expansive global food chain industry, controlled by dominant parties whose procurement standards and pricing determine how food is cultivated, sold and consumed. Their decisions have profound impacts on environmental (packaging, waste, emissions, logistics across the globe), health (food additives, quality and range of produce, animal welfare) and economic matters (livelihoods, work standards and safety, credit dependency and poverty).

A growing number of counter-reactions from unhappy or disadvantaged groups form the impetus for sustainable food chain transitions. These responses are part of complex *systems dynamics*, spontaneous and self-organized. Examples of shifts in behaviour are increasing consumption of natural and organic food; consumer demands for healthy and high-quality food; popularity of vegetarian and vegan trends; seasonal food consumption following; and growing push for local and regional food chains related to strengthening local economies.

Key features of complex systems dynamics characteristics include:

- Complex problems have multiple and varied dimensions, issues and parties, which are connected to each other and affect each other.
- Transitions, or response to complex systems imbalances are never predictable; they always lead to changes to existing paradigms and structural changes.
- There are always stakeholders who champion the *status quo*, who have much to gain by keeping things as they are; and others who push for new paradigms with the hope to gain with change.
- Reactions of self-organization and self-management dominate systems change; centralized decision-making and plans do not work;
- Complex *systems dynamics* cannot be solved by experts only, interactions between parties determine how change progresses; all parties are needed.
- Parallel developments take place in complex systems: simultaneous emergence of conflicting developments is possible.

Sensitivity is taking interconnectedness of systems into account and recognising that we can never map out or define every last detail of an entire system. We simply do not know what we do not know. What we can do is to pay attention to important issues and developments that are related, so that systemic patterns become visible.

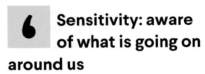 **Sensitivity: aware of what is going on around us**

Drawing *systems diagrams* is a good way to make patterns visible. We will illustrate this with a Dutch example of plagues of mice and weakening dykes. Dykes protect many of low-lying lands of the Netherlands. Parts of the country can be up to 7 metres below sea levels. Along rivers, dykes help with intermittent flooding risks along major rivers. Dyke maintenance and integrity is a major challenge where mice populations have grown. Mice loosen top-soil and affect the integrity of the dyke. The traditional intervention is to seal the weak spots created by mice with clay as and when this happens. Quick fixes of clay-filled holes are not effective as other factors are also at play: hard winds and high water. All three factors, mice, wind and high water, reinforce each other's effects on dykes.

A systems diagram captures how various elements interact and the resulting patterns. These patterns, in turn, help understand the need for other types of interventions than the initial response. In addition, including insights from multiple disciplines inevitably generate different interventions as opposed to when only 'normal' stakeholders are solving the problem. These ideas can initiate experimentation to identify viable ideas.

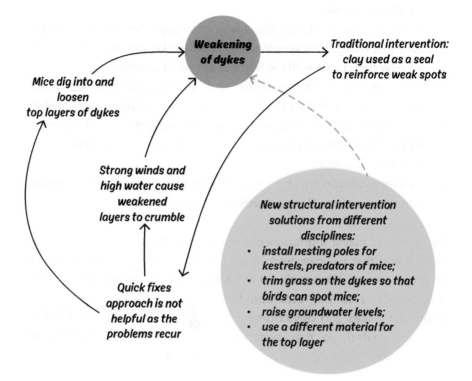

Drivers of change

Drivers of change are internal and external factors that exert influence on developments in a system. Some businesses depend strongly on new trends and developments for their continued existence; missing a new development or failing to keep pace with the competition can be fatal. *Haute couture*, the music industry and tech companies are such businesses. But even less trend-sensitive businesses can ill afford to ignore new developments.

Developing sensitivity for changes can be enhanced by recognizing *drivers of change* that influence shifts in the immediate circumstances or contexts.

Often, *drivers of change* include:

- demographic factors – immigration, ageing population, shrinking populations;
- environmental factors – climate change, pollution, resources depletion;
- politics and policy – new legislation, treaties and directives (UN/EU/NAFTA/ASEAN...), new political leadership;
- technological drivers – product innovations, dominance of mobile and digital platforms;
- economic and financial policy – recession, global trade, public-private partnerships;
- cultural developments – ethical shifts concerning major life issues and privacy.

It needs to be understood that *drivers of change* may be at a different systems level but affects systems at other levels as well: EU Green Deal directives affect national and regional policies but also all businesses. In addition, multiple *drivers of change* act simultaneously, and are mutually reinforcing, as is the case of gentrification of poor neighbourhoods: cheap air transport, rise of Airbnb, growing middle class, rise of digital platform technologies, growth of mass tourism, etc. Identifying *drivers of change* helps make explicit influences of drivers on systems developments. In designing systems interventions, *drivers of change* and their influences need to be taken into account.

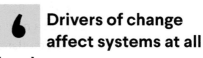 **Drivers of change affect systems at all levels**

Often, *drivers of change* are more important than focussing on the identity of systems in understanding complex problems. To illustrate, obesity has been recognized as a new epidemic in the Netherlands: one in ten Dutch persons meet the criteria for obesity. Rather than being viewed as a group with a collective identity, namely obese individuals, they are seen as individuals who do not exercise enough and eat too much. There are all kinds of societal factors, *drivers of change*, that play a role in the growing rate of obesity: advertising that encourages consumption; proximity and access to fast-food chains open 24 hours a day; hidden sugars in processed foods; limited physical exercise in schools and time devoted to sports; an increasingly sedentary lifestyles dominated by gaming, social media and binge watching on Netflix; usage of cars instead of cycling or walking, etc. These factors have as much an impact on individuals as genetic predispositions and the social milieu when growing up.

When obesity is defined at an individual problem, then solutions are sought for individuals. But even then, there is a tendency to address symptoms (diabetes, high cholesterol or high blood pressure), rather than treat them as being part of a larger condition. We have different specialists and specialist clinics for the different conditions, each with their own treatment plan. When individual cases reach critical thresholds of risks, or when patients can determine treatment plans, corrective surgery (gastric bypass, band or sleeve) with appropriate lifestyle change programmes may be chosen. These types of interventions will do nothing to alter the growing number of people with obesity.

Understanding *drivers of change* will guide the search for more effective systems interventions. The energy transition developments in the Netherlands can be linked to at least four *drivers of change* (Van Genus et al., 2017):
- Global warming due to the use of fossil fuels;
- Depletion of Dutch gas reserves;
- Earthquakes in Northern Netherlands due to extraction of gas;
- Consumer power.

These four *drivers of change* differ in terms of impact and time horizons: global warming in not a new phenomenon, its impact was gradual up to recent times. The Netherlands has been sluggish in its policy response to energy transition because their gas reserves were adequate. Tremors due to gas extraction were tolerated for a long time but more damaging earthquakes have increased the urgency to find alternative energy sources. Every new quake accelerates phasing out gas extraction earlier. Even so, political decision-making, long-term export contracts and political sensitivities of importing of gas play a role. Consumer power also influence the speed of energy transition developments. This example reveals how *drivers of change* related to the Dutch energy system are both from within and outside this system: shifts related to gas and consumer behaviours are from within, whilst climate change and earthquakes come from outside the energy system.

It is difficult to predict changes in complex systems. *Drivers of change* can play greater of lesser roles in changes: noticeable short-term effects are more effective in promoting awareness than long-term effects.

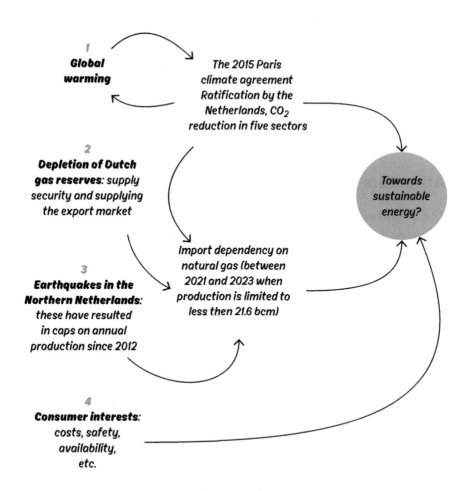

1
Global warming

The 2015 Paris climate agreement Ratification by the Netherlands, CO_2 reduction in five sectors

2
Depletion of Dutch gas reserves: supply security and supplying the export market

3
Earthquakes in the Northern Netherlands: these have resulted in caps on annual production since 2012

Import dependency on natural gas (between 2021 and 2023 when production is limited to less then 21.6 bcm)

Towards sustainable energy?

4
Consumer interests: costs, safety, availability, etc.

Weak signals

Weak signals are difficult to identify as these signals are at the fringes or outside the system, and whose relevance to the system is (as yet) unclear. A famous parable: when a frog is put into a pot of boiling water, it will jump out quickly, but if it is in the pot and the water is brought to boil slowly, it will not respond and die.[14] Thanks to our predispositions, we often fail to recognize *weak signals* until it is too late: when signals are outside our *bubble*, we do not see them coming.

 Weak signals are often overlooked

Weak signals pop up now and again and alerts us of possible developments. If we manage to step out of our *bubble*, we may be able

to detect emerging patterns or crises early on and act accordingly. It is easier to see how *weak signals* were present early in the process as forerunners of major shifts in systems with hindsight. For instance, will the growing number of vegetarians significantly impact global food chains? How will self-diagnostic trends and self-medication affect medical professionals and public health? We have seen how early warnings from scientists on the potential risk of pandemic virus outbreaks were ignored.

Attractors

The direction in which a dynamic system moves over time, despite opposing factors, is what we call '*attractors*' (Manickam, 2018). The term *attractor* comes from the field of mathematics and physics. The attractive force exerted by the sun and moon on the Earth is responsible for the movement of the tides. In dynamic systems theory, the concept of *attractor* is used to describe matters such as individualization, social justice and internationalization. Single-person households, mass tourism and populism are *attractors* as well. *Attractors* are unavoidable and irreversible despite resistance from numerous sides.

Dominant paradigms work as *attractors*. Liberal market economic paradigms have dominated modern societies in its economic policies and decision-making since the 80s. In addition, dominant globalization and digitalization shifts force us to become international and digital in our economic orientation and way of doing business. The 'new economic world' leaves us with little choice but to embrace new paradigms about businesses and trading.

Paradigm shifts do not occur seamlessly or without struggle. An existing dominant paradigm can come under pressure when it no longer serves its purpose of helping us understand reality or to justify how things are done. When that happens, new theories, ways of thinking and viewpoints arise, which may compete with existing paradigms and may nudge systems to move in a different direction, particularly, when such movements grow. Paradigms for understanding reality and structuring our lives determine not only how we think, but also how power, knowledge and money are distributed; and how physical, social and psychological structures in a society are organized. Paradigms influence how people treat one another and how discomfort or injustice is experienced.

Two competing paradigms

Traditional market economy	New economy
Competitive entrepreneurship: closed and independent	Collaborative networks: shared, open and interdependent
Shareholders, profit-driven	Stakeholders with diverse interests
Win-lose	Win-win
Values: beating competitors, profit maximisation, growth, speed	Values: economic, technological, ecological, sustainability
Producers and consumers	'Prosumers', social challenges, clusters
Hierarchical and pyramidal organization	Network organization
Authoritarian, rational, linear and hierarchical planning	Self-organization and emergent processes
Strategic goals determine tactical and operational goals	Goals emerge from interactive (*collective*) *sensemaking*
Strategy is analysis-based plans for the future	Strategy is flexible and opportunistic, reacting to changes in context
Organizational structure is rational, bureaucratic and functional	Organizational structure is flexible, dependent on prevailing shared goals
Aiming for homogeneity and uniformity in vision, structures and job specifications	Focus on variety and diversity: interdisciplinary and creative collaborations
Regulation, standardizing and creating protocols	Experimenting and learning from mistakes
Roles and responsibilities, tasks, authorization and accountability	Alignment, coherence and coordinated actions
Employees are replaceable and not independent: utilitarian relations	Partners are independent and have unique qualities: social relations
Control through processes, procedures and supervisors	Collaboration through trust, complementarity and results

Paul Verhaeghe, a Belgian psychoanalyst, explained in an article how neo-liberalism of the 20th century has created a system of competition with winners and losers, mutual distrust and individual entrepreneurship

(Verhaeghe, 2018). The competitive drive first emerged in the business world and later in other social arenas such as education, healthcare, football, etc. It has also led to more need for control, less social contracts based on trust, and this culminates in many lonely, fearful and depressed individuals.

An *attractor* such as neo-liberalism elicits a counter-reaction that seems to come out of nowhere. Those with dissimilar views, peripheral figures and victims of the system are the first to express dissent, which slowly gains traction as more people begin to identify with the 'dissenters'. The demand for a paradigm change gains momentum; allies to boost their cause are mobilized. Bottom-up movements, born of discontent, are a source of emergent, competing paradigms.

With regard to the economy, we currently find ourselves in a transition. The traditional market economy paradigm is dominant in society; commercialization has seeped into former public service sectors like education, healthcare, security, etc., but also to charities, arts and sports. The downsides of this paradigm have become increasingly evident, and can no longer be ignored: social equality, differences between rich and poor, is greater than ever; habitats for both people and animals have become inhospitable, threatened or irreversibly damaged; and Earth's capacity for recovery is under pressure. Economic norms measured in terms of money, growth and growth rates supress other norms such as health, happiness, self-sufficiency, notions of human and animal welfare, a sense of community and integrity of natural systems. Initial signs of a paradigm shift are increasingly evident.

Manifestations of a new economic paradigm are becoming visible:
- new cluster thinking broadening focus and scope on complex, social challenges, such as healthy ageing, sustainable mobility and forest bio-economy as well as embracing principles of circular and bio-based economy;
- bottom-up social movements: cooperatives in renewable energy and food in local communities;
- new networks of innovative businesses and business models reflecting shifting roles of consumers and producers;
- new paradigms related to product ownership: leased (and shared) bicycles, scooters, cars, appliances, etc.

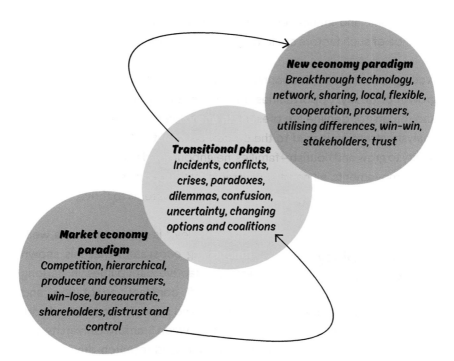

Responsivity

The responsivity of a system has to do not only with finding solutions for a changing environment, but also with developing a permanent ability to adapt to new circumstances.

When analyzing the *responsivity* of a system, we take five different aspects into account:

- ecosystems;
- fitness to landscape;
- differences that make the difference;
- self-organization;
- resilience and sustainability.

Ecosystems

An *ecosystem* is a context in which a community of stakeholders interact and engage with one another. Often, stakeholders interact to create meaningful value in order to promote growth and well-being. In a complex world, an adaptive *ecosystem* needs diversity, cohesion, competition, interactions, and influences from within and outside. The presence or absence of such factors could determine if growth or decay prevails.

A complex *ecosystem* is continuously developing. There is always change, growth or decay: opportunities for renewal or transition as well as risks and threats for decline are present. In analyzing *ecosystems* in a systems analysis, attention is paid to the contextual quality of the system and its ability to grow and flourish – families, neighbourhoods, businesses, regions, social movements, all need *ecosystems* that support their development, just as species need physical habitats and ecosystems to thrive.

6 *Responsivity*: a system's ability to adapt to changes

Silicon Valley[15] is an example of a well-functioning *ecosystem* that has shown strong adaptive capabilities in its long history of constant adaptation and change. In its system, learning, innovation and spin-offs go hand in hand. The fundamental strategy is strong links between Stanford University and the local industry. Stanford University prioritized research-driven spins-offs and strengthening local industry through new inventions. They created Science Parks to allow close collaborations on technology innovations and enterprise to thrive. Early on, federal contracts for research were also an important ingredient of its successful *ecosystem*. In later years, private capital, fluid mobility of knowledge, talent and resources, risk and failure tolerance were also part of the ecosystem that fostered its rapid growth but also its ability to rebound when things were difficult.

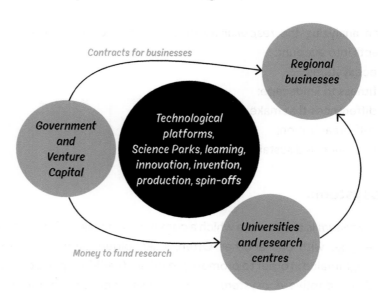

Responsivity is about constantly adapting to new circumstances. Despite its consistent success, Silicon Valley must remain alert. The *Silicon Valley Competitiveness and Innovation Project – 2017 Report*[16] provided clear evidence that, while the region continued to grow more quickly than other regions in the United States and that number of innovations continues to increase, there were concerns. Venture capitalists were making fewer investments; cost of living has been exorbitantly high; travel expenses of commuters were becoming unmanageable; residents were leaving, fewer entrepreneurs are choosing to locate in the area; and the quality of high school education was declining. Silicon Valley had failed to respond to signals (weak or otherwise) from in and outside the system adequately.

A different example to illustrate *responsivity* of an *ecosystem*: the case of a rural village faced with declining amenities and population, common to less thriving rural communities. The residents launched a number of initiatives to enhance the attractiveness of the village. Together with the municipality and the social housing corporation, residents explored ways to increase the pool of homes available for first-time home owners. The goal was to attract young people to the village. Next, a solar-energy meadow, a wind turbine for communal facilities and more sport facilities were realized. When the village supermarket threw in the towel, the residents established a village co-operative to run the shop. Other initiatives included restoring the community centre and converting the local Christian school to one open to students of all faiths. Finally, the village also acted pro-actively with a timely response to planned infrastructural changes imposed by provincial authorities. The plans would have adversely affected the village. The village clearly displayed an *adaptive ecosystem*, alert to changes from within and outside its system and capable of prompt and effective measures for its continued growth and development.

Fitness to landscape

Fitness to landscape (Manickam, 2018) is the co-evolution and alteration of a system to ensure its continued alignment to a changing landscape. This requires capabilities that are appropriate to the changed landscape. We see multiple shifts in the current landscape. One example is Massive Open Online Courses (MOOC) that offer online educational courses to thousands of participants globally. How do educational institutions and individual lecturers respond to such developments? Another example is the trend towards *personalized and preventive healthcare*: How will traditional healthcare systems respond? Will they co-evolve to fit this shift? We see businesses responding by offering healthcare kits and products to allow individuals to monitor and self-medicate various health conditions. Gyms and other fitness centres are offering new services like personal trainers and dedicated programmes for target groups. Will health systems and general practioners adapt to these changing patterns of patients and social trends?

❛ Co-evolution to fit the changing landscape

Fitness to landscape adaptations are not a given. Too often, changes progress so rapidly that regions, businesses, but also groups and individuals, are not able to adapt on time.

- Major department stores and retails chains: Blockbuster Video, Toys 'r Us, Laure Ashley, Tower Records, Borders, but also other businesses, Nokia, Kodak, etc., were too slow to respond to changing competition and consumer behaviours.
- Manufacturing industries are confronted by the notion of 'Industry 4.0', shaped by the Internet of Things, Artificial Intelligence, robotics and digital platforms, which will radically alter production processes.
- Car mechanics, highly knowledgeable in engine technology, are at risk of losing their jobs if they lack skills in electronics and computerized car technology; and with further advances in the 'car', 'driverless cars' rely on different types of technical support where sensors, integrated circuits, battery and other modern systems dominate what constitutes a 'car' and therefore the support services needed.

Recent studies have shown that around 60% of professions will see at least 30% per cent of their tasks automated and 5% could be completely automated.[18] An article published on the World Economic Forum's website indicates that while 82% of executives intend to implement artificial intelligence in their companies, only 38% are working on programmes to prepare their employees (Tyagarajan, 2018).[19]

The rapidly changing workplace has also raised questions on the educational offerings of schools. Learning cannot stop at school; lifelong learning is the creed. Are schools able to prepare students with competences that support flexibility and adaptability for responding to rapidly changing contexts? Communication, social and emotional skills will be prioritised in the future. Jobs in healthcare and education will continue to exist, as will upper-level professions which require extensive problem-solving ability and creativity. Schools must teach young people to be creative in how they arrange their lives. They must prepare pupils for the myriad new challenges – such as automation, artificial intelligence, cyberthreats and privacy risks – that make the future uncertain and give rise to security issues and ethical dilemmas. In a *wicked world*, the emphasis is increasingly on doing what inspires you and acquiring expertise in the process.

Differences that make the difference

'Meaningful differences' are variations that yield better outcomes than the commonly accepted answers.[20] In 1972, Gregory Bateson explained '*a difference which makes a difference*' - a new idea can make a difference between flourishing and decay. Systems survive when they are able to respond differently in differing situations. Having a broad spectrum of possible responses is vital, as this offers more options for effective response to new situations. Increasingly, students in the Netherlands are opting for Bachelor programmes that are more generic and broad-based to give them more career options. Specialized programmes were up to recently, the preferred option.

Many things can make a meaningful difference. If lost in the jungle, a knife or a bottle of water can mean the difference between life and death; an emerging industry can change an entire sector; a new method of collaboration can impact an entire region. However, not every change will make a meaningful difference: adding fifty random individuals to your digital network can be less meaningful than adding one person who can change your career or life perspectives.

Sometimes, a small incident can have major consequences. This is known as the 'butterfly effect'.[21] Changes at a local level may lead to developments 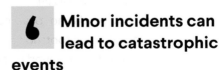 **Minor incidents can lead to catastrophic events** on larger scale. The Arab Spring Movement began in Tunisia in 2010 when Mohammed Bouazizi set himself on fire as a protest against police violence and the government, which then sparked the Jasmine Revolution. Citizens protested against the president, censorship in Tunisia, high food prices and widespread unemployment. The success of this protest inspired movements in other Middle-Eastern countries including Egypt, Bahrain, Iran, Syria and Libya. These events impacted the entire world, as new coalitions of nations and parties were formed. Islamic State (IS) gained in strength in the region, leading to repression. The series of events added to the growing strength of terrorists' threats worldwide.

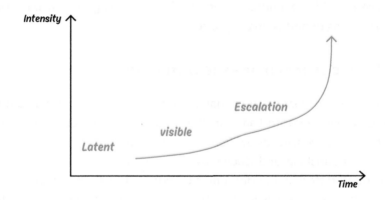

Paying attention to the presence of *differences that matter* is critical, to ensure broad and integral perspectives on the entire landscape. When insufficient diversity prevails, severe consequences can result: A new city near Delhi, Gurgaon, arose from private initiatives.[22] Within 30 years, over 1.5 million inhabitants were housed. However, the government was not involved and each project developer was preoccupied with their own project only. The result was a city that was extremely attractive to wealthy and highly-educated people who wanted to live in large, secure housing compounds. Around these gated communities, however, arose slums housing the original inhabitants and new migrants working in nearby business parks and for the new wealthy residents. Five-star hotels, luxury shopping centres and golf courses were plentiful, but public infrastructure was limited. The result was that slums were riddled with potholed roads; no pavements anywhere because the wealthy never go anywhere on foot; no sewer system was installed; limited police patrols as gated compounds and business parks employed private security firms; etc. Each housing development had its own facilities: diesel generators for electricity; septic tanks for toilets; and private firms collecting trash, although no one was keeping track of where that rubbish ends up. Groundwater was pumped up, with no thought to how this may affect the water supply for the city as a whole. A small difference, the lack of government involvement, in this case created a system built to fail on many levels.

Self-organization

Birds, ants, people, businesses all pursue their own goals whilst interacting with others in their environment, also in pursuit of their own goals. Collectively, their behaviours create patterns of *self-organization*, whilst pursuing individual goals.

Heylighen (2009) captures this as '*self-organization can be defined as the spontaneous emergence of global structure out of local interactions*'. *Self-organization* arises when local interaction occurs, but the resulting patterns are visible on a higher plane. *Self-organizing* patterns are seen in classrooms, in families, during revolutions, in parliament, across a region, etc.

A good example of *self-organization* is evident at a busy traffic junction in a city like Mumbai. Traffic seems chaotic, overcrowded with very different types of vehicles (auto rikshaw, scooters, lorries, cars, busses) but also pedestrians and cows, sharing limited space and often with inadequate or non-functioning formal traffic signs (traffic lights, traffic police, signs, right-of-way signage, segregated paths for different kinds of traffic). There is a lot going on: pedestrians crossing the street, scooters in a rush to get home, cars avoid hitting a drunken man or cows grazing along the sides, overcrowded busses have passengers hanging out of the door, but also everyone inching through criss-crossing of traffic as **Simple rules support self-organization** they manoeuvre through 2 or 3 lanes to get to their turn-off. It looks chaotic but there is some order in all of this. Everyone pays attention to what the others are doing; they communicate to other parties through honking or gesturing; if needed, they brake, or accelerate, and sometimes by ignoring the others if they can get away with it. The cows, sacred, are never hurt. It feels counter-intuitive, but it works because they all want to move on, *simple rules* emerge and this makes *self-organization* possible.

Simple rules and patterns of success evolve with new developments. For instance: at first, accidents at the intersection are frequent because situations can be interpreted in multiple ways and communication is poor. Through trial and error, interactions and learning, patterns of behaviour and interactions become more effective. Patterns of behaviour in traffic in chaotic situations are different everywhere in the world: through different use of car horns, flashing headlights or gestures or other devices. *Simple rules* emerge to allow *self-organization.*

Trends emerge when patterns of success spread across the world, often, with increasing speed and frequency due to globalisation and social media. Also, past patterns are quickly replaced when new improvements come along.

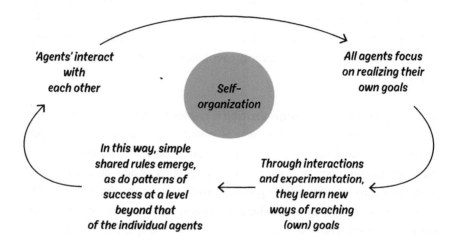

Self-organization is specific to certain types of circumstances:
- crises;
- poorly managed or organized situations;
- in complex and rapidly-changing environments;
- in rigidly structured top-down organizations where individual interests are supressed;
- where unclear boundaries and principles exist.

Self-organization requires parameters, codes and rules in order to flourish. In the absence of external control mechanisms, rules are flaunted: the Roman Catholic Church was infested with sexual abuse of youth due to its isolation; the financial crisis in 2008 and 2009 led to a currency crisis in Europe due to the failure of financial regulators.

Resilience and sustainability

Resilience is the ability to 'bounce back' to a good condition or position quickly after encountering problems, and to adapt or transform when necessary. The question is whether a system is crisis-proof, and whether it will be able to sustain itself socially, ecologically and economically in the long-term.

The literature offers varying definitions of *resilience*. Bristow and Healy (2015) define '*resilience*' as how shock-proof a system is and how

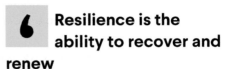

Resilience is the ability to recover and renew

quickly that system is able to recover after a shock. But also, its ability to continually innovate and to reorient when the context changes. The latter has to do with the sustainability of a system.

Bristow and Healy's definition resembles that of Béné et al. (2012), who distinguish three ways for a system to maintain its *resilience*:

- *Absorptive coping capacity*: how a system maintains itself and recovers following a shock. This typically pertains to shocks of a small, one-off nature: floods, market fluctuations and death in a family are some examples.
- *Adaptive capacity*: the ability of a system to keep up with the times and adapt to changing circumstances, and applies to all systems levels: the COVID-19 pandemic changed the world we lived in dramatically and we had to adapt. Governments were led by scientists; new rules were created: lockdown, masks and social distancing. Personal tests to check personal resilience emerged '*Test your own COVID-19 Resilience at http://www.thtconsulting. com/Covid-19/#/.*'
- *Transformative capacity*: drastic and far-reaching changes that have the potential to alter entire systems completely. This usually involves a combination of technological innovations, institutional reforms and cultural/behavioural changes. For instance, the rise of the Internet profoundly changed our lives.

Kathleen Sutcliffe (2017) provides specific recommendations for promoting the *resilience* of a system. These include:
- Treat everyone as being competent and capable of goodwill in all sincerity.

- Emphasize that there are no simple solutions.
- Be alert to small things going wrong as it happens and restructure processes immediately if needed.
- Be focussed on the front line and give timely and ample support – that is where it all happens.
- Nurture face-to-face contact to harvest 'rich' details.
- Think and pose questions aloud and encourage others to do so.
- Listen to each other's opinions and encourage ideas that differ.
- Share knowledge and encourage others to do so about what is going on.
- Give the power to those knowledgeable of the issue to decide; many times, this is *not* the company's top brass.
- Allow self-organization.

To enhance coping with external shocks and sustained *resilience*, we supplement Sutcliffe's list with the following:
- *Prepare for the worst*: organize large-scale emergency response drills before a calamity strikes; subject banks to a stress test; build dykes when the sea level rises.
- *Create loosely connected systems* : a bicycle consists of separate components that can be replaced individually; when every household generates its own energy through solar panels, widespread blackouts are of the past.
- *Make sure there is a back-up plan*: prevent immediate collapse of systems with emergency generators in hospitals; having two pilots and two engines per aircraft; reservoirs to provide water during droughts.
- *Avoid excessive austerity measures*: cutting costs can have harmful consequences; 30,000 additional deaths occurred in 2014 and 2015 in the UK due to massive cutbacks to the NHS.[23] It is difficult to determine critical thresholds for cost-cutting in advance, and attempting to perch right on the threshold of acceptability yields risks.
- *Keep multiple options open and avoid betting all your money on one horse*: many businesses have a mix of permanent, temporary, and flexible employment contracts in order to remain flexible; businesses have multiple products and multiple sources of suppliers to ensure spread of vulnerability and risks.
- *Experiment first*: set up pilot projects before overhauling an entire system, for example, convert one department to an open-plan office and only remodel the rest if the experiences are positive.

- *Look for connections*: businesses should connect to broader social and technological trends. In a *wicked world*, creativity and innovative ability of students should be a priority in education, to make them ready for their roles in a complex world; businesses need to connect to shifting consumer trends of demanding sustainability, locally sourced produce, organic and slave-free produce, etc.; research funding, needs to follow suit. In 2018, the Dutch government earmarked funding for 25 research tracks through the Netherlands Organization for Scientific Research (NWO) as part of its National Science Agenda.[24] The Agenda aims to solve complex societal challenges and bring about transformative capacity for individuals and society as a whole.

Connectivity

Systems always change in conjunction with other systems.[25] *Connectivity* deals with the connections between systems and the link to new themes and other systems levels.

This applies to any system, including isolated systems. An island in the middle of the ocean is subject to change due to the influence of other systems such as the weather, the flora and fauna present, and all their complex interactions.

When considering *connectivity* as a component of a systems analysis, there are five key concepts to remember:

- co-evolution;
- transformative interactions;
- networking;
- societal developments;
- cross-border connections.

Co-evolution

Co-evolution is a concept drawn from the field of biology. Ehrlich and Raven (1964) used this concept to describe the interaction and resulting symbiotic developments between butterflies and flowering plants. Butterflies and flowering plants co-evolve in a sustainable and mutually profitable process.

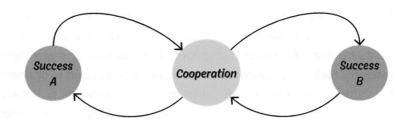

Co-evolution can also be observed in more complex phenomena as economic clusters. Porter (2003) refers to a cluster as a '*geographically proximate group of interconnected companies, suppliers, service providers and associated institutions in a particular field, linked by externalities of various types*'. According to Delgado et al. (2014), strong clusters offer major advantages: the growth of employment is greater than elsewhere; wages are higher; productivity is higher; more new businesses decide to settle there and the number of patents requested and received is above average. In addition, strong clusters benefit from the presence of other strong clusters in the same region, as was the case in the Karlstad region, Sweden.

Clusters are associated with what is known as the 'triple helix'. Etzkowitz (2000) introduced this concept in 1993 as a means of describing the relationships between universities, industries and governments. Each 'helix' serves a different function: universities foster research and education; local governments and regional management agencies are custodians of public safety and welfare; and businesses pursue wealth creation and create employment. These helixes, through joint activities and commitment to fostering the economic cluster's purpose, can become more innovative, both separately and collectively, through the creation of a knowledge-driven innovation ecosystem. This, in turn, will enhance the prosperity of the entire community. More recently cluster experts and policymakers refer to *quadruple and quintuple helix*, to acknowledge the role of civil society and financial institutions in the co-evolution of modern cluster developments.

> **❛** *Co-evolution:* **systems never evolve independently of other systems**

Co-evolution is not always productive and positive. One example of this is the 'arms race' whereby countries build their military arsenals, including nuclear power, as they feel threatened by their opponents, who in turn, increase their military and nuclear capacities – resulting in an escalating process.

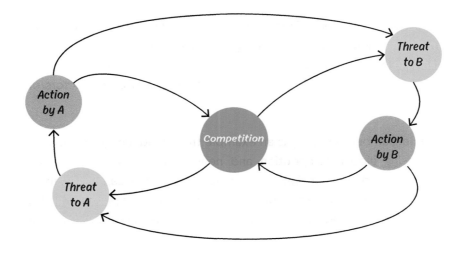

Similar patterns are present when competing supermarkets and retail outlets resort to price wars in the battle for customers.

Transformative interactions

Transformative interactions are interactions that change systems. For example, the #MeToo movement has changed relationships between men and women. Similarly, conversations between the then recently freed Nelson Mandela, on behalf of African National Congress, and the then president of South Africa, de Klerk, eventually led to the end of apartheid.

Transformative interactions can also take place when new systems are introduced: mobile and digital communications and social media

Transformative interactions change systems

have changed how human beings interact and how things are done. Governments, tax authorities, the educational sector, the media, politicians, the healthcare sector, etc., have websites and on-line portals for information or personal interactions with these agencies; professionals but also individuals, are using digital gadgets like Fitbit and other wearables to measure their fitness abilities and keep track of their health; digital communities are arising based on shared interests or experiences, exchanging information and personal details without knowing each other 'in real life'.

Transformative interactions may occur in a wide variety of arenas. Traditional industries that are struggling as a result of global competition can take on a new life by linking themselves to new technologies; new ways of organizing their production processes; and other sectors or disciplines.

The Belgian beer industry is an example that faced a major crisis with increasing global competition and new beer trends.[26] Well-known Belgian brands include Leffe, Lambiek, Trappist, Geuze, Hoegaarden, Duvel and Stella. Belgian beer always had a high reputation and a considerable market share in Europe. However, a decline in consumption resulted due to:

- new entrants to the market: Indian, Scandinavian, American, British and Dutch beers;
- competitors' innovations: new flavours, brewing techniques, recipes and packaging;
- new trends of customer engagement: via social media and crowdfunding for investments.

Changes in the beer market pushed Belgian brewers to learn from their customers and competitors: they connected to specific target groups; listened to consumers; and connected to creative industries to improve brand image and packaging. This resulted in creating new local and speciality beers and digital 'beer communities'; decisions to include new sources of raw materials of malt, hops, coffee, fruit, wood, spices and water; and priority to R&D, brewery design, quality standards, bottling plants, labelling facilities, packaging, shipping, restaurants and consumers.

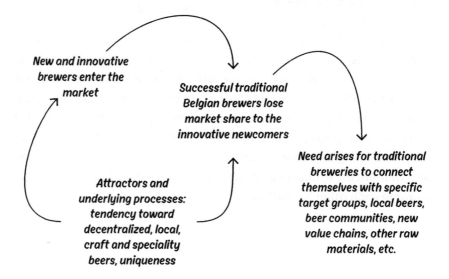

New and innovative brewers enter the market

Successful traditional Belgian brewers lose market share to the innovative newcomers

Need arises for traditional breweries to connect themselves with specific target groups, local beers, beer communities, new value chains, other raw materials, etc.

Attractors and underlying processes: tendency toward decentralized, local, craft and speciality beers, uniqueness

Networks

Networking used to be an informal aspect one's professional practice in businesses, political organizations and movements. Today, however, *networking* is critical to do business, tackle problems, become part of a group and mobilize groups for advocacy. For complex challenges, multi and trans disciplinary networks are vital in the search for effective interventions.

Digital platforms have changed and simplified how we *network*. Instagram, LinkedIn, Facebook, YouTube, Snapchat and Twitter make

❝ Networks bring positive value, but also have downsides

it possible to establish contacts all over the world with just a few clicks. With each new contact our *network* grows exponentially. *Networks* are valuable when they add reliable knowledge and new contacts, but like every new system that is introduced, they also have a downside: hackers, spyware, identity theft, spam, violation of privacy, reputation damage, fake news, mass manipulation, personal activities and movements assessible to friends, stalkers, criminals, etc.

Networking can lead to innovation; and you can deploy your *networks* to implement interventions. Even as parties within a given *network* may have differing interests, they usually have a common focus or shared objective. A *network* knows more, can do more and sees more than any of its individual members. Intuitively, members of the *network* know what needs to happen and what unique contribution they can offer.

There are different types of *networks*, some examples are:
- alliances between entrepreneurs as part of a value chain;
- regional clusters or hubs in which various parties, governments, businesses, residents, innovation centres, banks, etc., cooperate on specific themes or based on sectors: sustainable mobility and paper industry;
- local organizations working together in a network, task force or cooperative to tackle complex social issues: preserving natural or cultural landscapes, rejuvenating traditional crafts and addressing youth unemployment;

- swarms as part of a military operation, in which various units and technical tools are mobilized for combat or intelligence purposes: communication, flexibility and mutual coordination are of vital importance in such unpredictable and dangerous situations;
- networks cooperating at different system levels: European networks working with national and regional networks on education, immigration, corruption, etc., and the 100 Resilient Cities network joining forces to become robust and sustainable;
- interdisciplinary collaborations between researchers and innovators globally, combating persistent problems like poverty, environmental disasters, Zika, Ebola, and COVID-19.

Forming an effective *network* demands certain competencies of all participants. These include but are not limited to: flexibility, trust, willingness to learn, ability to communicate, willingness to adopt a shared vision or paradigm, decisiveness, self-organization, shared leadership and taking responsibility for managing some parts.

Engaging with societal challenges

Connectivity means engaging with the larger community and its developments.

Connecting to societal challenges has become increasingly vital in our complex world, as everything is interconnected. Businesses are increasingly coming to terms with the fact that societal challenges are not limited to politics and governments, but that they too carry responsibility for them and that everyone is a stakeholder when it comes to climate change, immigration, terrorism, social justice, etc. New *connectivity* emerges between networks organized around social themes are connected, and that businesses can connect to such networks to connect but also harness these challenges to develop viable business models whilst serving the common good.

In the past, key Dutch corporations like Philips and Stork understood the significance of connectivity early in their development.[27] It is what made them successful in their time. Philips and Stork knew that they needed to be valuable to their respective communities in order to thrive. In 1910, Philipsdorp was constructed in Eindhoven, a village built specifically to house Philips employees that had its own vegetable plots, bakery, pharmacy and sports field. That sports field eventually grew into the Philips Sport Vereniging (PSV), a major Dutch football club. Avid fans and loyal employees were the result of their endeavour to connect with the community. Similarly, in Hengelo, Stork created the garden village of 't Lansink for its personnel with a library, bathhouse and clubhouse for residents. Other recent examples, IKEA, Netflix, Lego, Michelin, Bill Gates (Microsoft), Nespresso, Unilever, Apple, to name a few, have chosen to connect to one or more social issues such as reducing carbon footprints, changing industry standards on labour, embracing fair trade and circular economy principles.

However, multiple examples of companies, blinded by profit and short-term targets, completely lost sight of the interests of their local communities. Examples are: the successful Schiphol International Airport, a major aviation hub, focussed on growth, ignored increasing noise and air pollution and the impact of its fuel usage on climate change; major clothing and manufacturing corporations relocating to low-wage countries to improve their bottom lines at the expense of poor labour conditions and long-haul transportation contributing to social injustice, poverty and carbon emissions. In addition, companies flooding cities in third world countries are disrupting local economies.

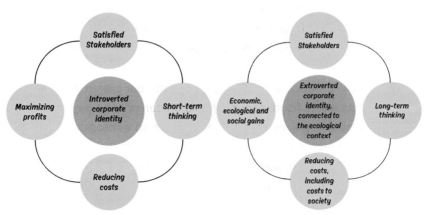

The major effects businesses exert on other systems is becoming increasingly clear. Taking other interests such as social and ecological well-being into account should be a fixed component of every business' corporate strategy. Social entrepreneurs are already applying this new market ideology to tackle major social issues in innovative ways (Goldstein et al., 2009).

In an article in the *Harvard Business Review*, Michael Porter and Mark Kramer (2011) call for businesses to redefine their objectives. They champion the idea of shared value as a corporate strategy: becoming more successful yourself by improving the economic and social conditions in the communities in which your company operates. Corporate interests can easily go hand-in-hand with the interests of the community: conserving water, promoting safety and health, developing the professional skills of employees, using sustainable energy and so on. Multinationals trading in commodities such as tea, cacao, coffee, bananas, fish, etc., or trading or manufacturing through global production chains, have had to commit to (increased) adherence and accountability for fair, sustainable and ethical practices throughout their supply chain. Fair trade and good stewardship certifications and recently, social impact benchmarking are developments that are moving businesses towards societally responsible practice. Aaron Hurst (2018) foresees a revolutionary shift as a new economic era driven by 'purpose' emerges, in which personal, professional and organizational purpose will frame future developments.

Engage for societal profits

Kate Raworth takes this idea a step further. In her book *Doughnut Economics: Seven Ways to Think Like a 21st-Century Economist*, Raworth describes how the focus on economic growth has led to extreme inequality between people and an ecological disaster (2017). She proposes an entirely different kind of economy aimed at meeting everyone's basic needs within the possibilities our planet offers. Basic needs such as water, food, energy and so on can only be met in a social economy that recognizes that our planet has an ecological ceiling. In the space between meeting minimum basic needs and the ecological threshold lies urgent challenges to transform current practice to make ensure sustainable and equitable futures.

The drive to attain social and ecological well-being is also reflected in the Sustainable Development Goals for 2015-2030[28] established by the United Nations (UN). These guidelines apply to all countries and all people. They serve to inspire entrepreneurs, individuals and countries to make the social and ecological well-being of all people and nature into account when developing corporate, personal and policy strategies.

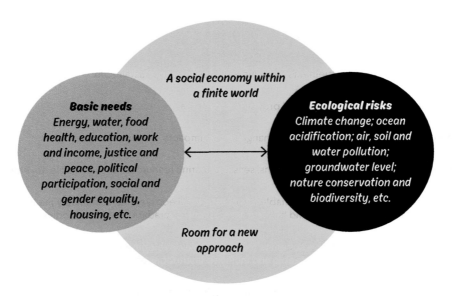

A social economy within
a finite world

Basic needs
*Energy, water, food
health, education, work
and income, justice and
peace, political
participation, social and
gender equality,
housing, etc.*

Ecological risks
*Climate change; ocean
acidification; air, soil and
water pollution;
groundwater level;
nature conservation and
biodiversity, etc.*

Room for a new
approach

The UN Sustainable Development Goals

- End poverty in all its forms everywhere

- End hunger, achieve food security and improved nutrition and promote sustainable agriculture

- Ensure healthy lives and promote well-being for all at all ages

- Ensure inclusive and equitable quality education and promote lifelong learning opportunities for all

- Achieve gender equality and empower all women and girls

- Ensure availability and sustainable management of water and sanitation for all

- Ensure access to affordable, reliable, sustainable and modern energy for all

- Promote sustained, inclusive and sustainable economic growth, full and productive employment and decent work for all

- Build resilient infrastructure, promote inclusive and sustainable industrialization, and foster innovation

- Reduce inequality within and among countries

- Make cities and human settlements inclusive, safe, resilient and sustainable

- Ensure sustainable consumption and production patterns

- Take urgent action to combat climate change and its impacts

- Conserve and sustainably use the oceans, seas and marine resources for sustainable development

- Protect, restore and promote sustainable use of terrestrial ecosystems, sustainably manage forests, combat desertification and halt and reverse land degradation and halt biodiversity loss

- Promote peaceful and inclusive societies for sustainable development, provide access to justice for all and build effective, accountable and inclusive institutions at all levels

- Strengthen the means of implementation and revitalize the global partnership for sustainable development

Boundary crossing links

In a complex world, survival means being willing to transcend borders. *Wicked problems* are not impeded by borders. They ignore boundaries between departments, organizations; and transcend knowledge disciplines, specializations and sectors. To effectively address *wicked problems*, you need a variety of perspectives and paradigms; cross boundaries and assume the following:

- Systems always exist in relation to other systems and other system levels.
- It is possible to transcend scientific disciplines and professions, their theories and jargon.
- Societal divisions, cultures, hierarchies, positions and roles can be transcended.
- Ethnic background, sex and age are enrichments, not limitations.

On 26 September 2017, a vacuum cleaner manufacturer, James Dyson wrote the following memo[29] to his employees: *'It has remained my ambition to find solutions to the global problem of air pollution. Some years ago, observing that automotive firms were not changing their spots, I committed the company to develop new battery technologies. I believed that electrically powered vehicles would solve the vehicle pollution problem. Dyson carried on innovating. The latest digital motors and energy storage systems power the Dyson Supersonic hair dryer and cord-free vacuum line. We have relentlessly innovated in fluid dynamics and HVAC systems to build our fans, heaters, and purifiers. At this moment, we finally have the opportunity to bring all our technologies together into a single product. Rather than filtering emission at the exhaust pipe, today we have the ability to solve it at the source. So I wanted you to hear it directly from me: Dyson has begun work on a battery electric vehicle, due to be launched by 2020.'*

Changes in systems can emerge from cross-boundary linkages and transcending differences between separate structures, knowledge and professional specializations, cultures and systems levels.

In conclusion

To instigate *systems innovation*, a thorough system analysis is needed. Understanding the dynamics of complex problems, how they emerge and persist, will help the search for potential interventions. The *systems analysis framework* offers a systems tool for mapping *wicked problems*: we can define the *identity* of a given system; explore its *sensitivity* to its internal and external contextual changes; gauge its *response* to such changes; and how it achieves *connectivity* to create appropriate solutions in cooperation with other systems and agents.

3

Systems innovation

An analysis of a system's *identity*, *sensitivity*, *responsivity* and *connectivity* is the start of systems intervention; working together with stakeholders initiates the change process. Interventions influence systems dynamics and therefore paths of development. Trust and shared perspectives are important elements of systems innovation. How can we increase trust? How do we transcend differences to create common purpose in a constantly changing world? How do we successfully mobilize others? Smart interventions require new ways of thinking, communicating, engaging and doing.

Systems innovation framework

Systems innovation is working collectively to address major challenges: complex challenges that have no apparent solutions at hand, where opinions differ on definitions of the problem, but also, how to solve it. Even good solutions are likely to meet resistance by one or more parties. Therefore, it is important to focus on building alliances, collaborations, understanding those with differing or opposing views to seek common ground.

The framework for *systems innovation* focuses on creating collaborative milieus with four focal pillars:
- upholding mutual trust, transparency and integrity;
- developing shared awareness and perspective;
- designing and effecting smart interventions together;
- mobilizing allies for change.

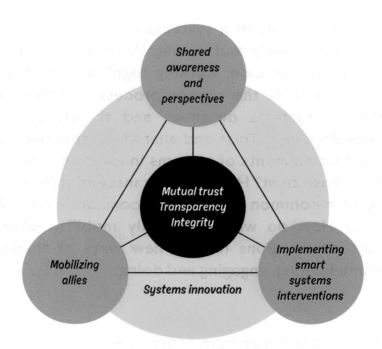

Trust, transparency and integrity

Systems innovation is not achieved alone. We need to work together to prompt systems changes. Trust, transparency and integrity are prerequisites for collaboration.

Trust manifests itself through *transparent* conduct; the *integrity* of the parties involved; reliability and voluntary involvement. *Trust* occurs between individuals; between groups; and between individuals, groups, organizations and institutions.

LaRue Tone Hosmer (1995) defines trust as follows: '*Trust is the reliance by one person, group, or firm upon a voluntarily accepted duty on the part of another person, group, or firm to recognize and protect the rights and interests of all others engaged in a joint endeavour of economic exchange.*' He advocates that trust is more than a naively optimistic belief that everything will work out fine. This also excludes behaviour by parties who are occupied solely with their own interests, with rigid contracts with other parties to defend such interests. Trust is found in all aspects of society, not only in economic transactions.

Trust, transparency and *integrity*, are essential constituents of the new economic paradigm where stakeholders rely on one another. In an extensive study on economic clusters, Anu Manickam (2018) identified emerging patterns of cooperation whereby trust and engagement were central, and this was for all systems levels: cluster, regional, national and European. Patterns of collaborations and behaviours in social movements, neighbourhood care, cooperatives and open innovation networks are strengthened.

 Trust is key in the new economic paradigm

In the new economic paradigm, initiatives, founded on principles of *trust, transparency* and *integrity*, are governed by a few simple rules:

- Everyone who participates is taken seriously, regardless of their viewpoint and vested interests.
- Exploring differences is important to get a good understanding of the problem and to analyse it effectively.
- Everyone can express themselves freely, subject to checks of validity.
- The process is more important than outcomes.
- Everyone plays an active part.
- Dialogue – listening, responding, cooperating – is more important than discussion – arguments, polemics, competition.

Shared awareness and perspectives

By entering a dialogue, we can broaden our own perspective and work towards a common vision. A prerequisite for dialogue is open-minds, curiosity and mutual trust. This in turn, increases *shared awareness* and new *perspectives*. This is known as *collective sensemaking*.

Collective sensemaking

Collective sensemaking[30] is a shared process of understanding events and developments in a *wicked world. Sensemaking* is an active process – by doing, by interacting – we discover what is happening and whether our actions make *sense*.

Complex challenges are unpredictable as they are constantly changing. Investigating *wicked problems* is different to solving problems that are *'tame'* where facts, trends and expertise support effective solutions development. In the *wicked problems*, facts and information on developments tell us a lot about past and present conditions of the problems but cannot resolve them because the future is unknown. Many factors, known and unknown, influence such problems, including perceptions, interests and behaviours of those involved.

Sensemaking is shared awareness and perspectives

Collective sensemaking is the way forward. Carrying out small interventions and experiments and seeing what happens, helps us find answers and workable solutions sooner. '*The basic idea of sensemaking is that reality is an ongoing accomplishment that emerges from efforts to create order and make retrospective sense of what occurs*' (Weick, 1993).

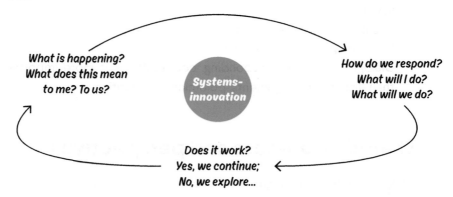

What is happening?
What does this mean
to me? To us?

Systems-
innovation

How do we respond?
What will I do?
What will we do?

Does it work?
Yes, we continue;
No, we explore...

Properties of *sensemaking* according to Weick (1995):
- **Identity and identification** are important as people construe their identity from the behaviour of others, react to what is happening and decide how to interpret events.
- **Retrospection** is important to *sensemaking*; it allows us to understand what happened, especially when we are focussed on making sense.
- Dialogues and interactions help us **enact** (endorse) the circumstances around us – talking about events help us clarify our thoughts, order our experiences, provide a grasp of what is happening and make it workable.

- *Sensemaking* is a **social activity** whereby we create a continuously-evolving story about reality, for ourselves individually and collectively with others.
- *Sensemaking* is **ongoing**: individuals react as well as shape events happening around them, and constantly verify their identity and views of the world.
- **Selecting cues** from the context helps us choose what information is relevant, which interpretations are plausible and how to connect to developments at large.
- We prefer **plausibility over accuracy** in narratives about events and circumstances to be able to deal with ambiguous and complex worlds.

Collective sensemaking needs to meet four conditions to be successful.

1 Choose challenging problems or issues

To start, begin with a definition of the chosen challenge and make sure that the scope is not too narrow or too broad. Also, make sure that the problem definition invites stakeholders to participate. Defining the problems of urban growth needs to be different for Cape Town as opposed to London. Each city has its own challenges and priorities: townships and slums are relevant aspects for Cape Town but not for London; exorbitant property prices are critical to London's urban problems.

2 Involve pertinent stakeholders

Identifying which stakeholders are relevant will depend on the preliminary definition of the problem. Ensure that there is a representation of stakeholders with varying standpoints, interests, roles and resources. In the urbanisation example, the following stakeholders may be relevant: residents, municipality, government agencies, project owners and developers, investors, businesses from different sectors, interest groups, etc. In Cape Town, but also in London, different neighbourhoods may have different impacts of urbanization and therefore different stakeholder groups need to be involved.

3 Transcend dialogues to outcomes

To facilitate *collective sensemaking*, we have to ensure a continued dialogue of high quality. An article from Boersma and Lohman (2018) published in the Dutch newspaper *de Volkskrant*, illustrates how difficult this can be. In the article, proponents of two different viewpoints discuss what the future of agriculture should look like. The interviewees attempted to transcend the binary conflict between 'ecologists' (traditional food growers, biodiversity and nature-inclusive agriculture) and 'technologists' (technologically-advanced, intensive agriculture) as they understood the need for increased food production, healthier and more sustainable food and food chains. However, the supporters of the two groups continue in their conflict on how to solve food production and defend their standpoints. The result is a stagnated debate.

4 Visualize using rich pictures

By using *rich pictures* to visualize the different stories, stakeholder interests are made explicit and a better overview of how elements of various systems relate to one another is realized. Drawing *systems diagrams* help identify the need to subject assumptions to further scrutiny. Creating a rich picture of urbanisation challenges of Amsterdam as shown below could help the municipality and other stakeholders to have a dialogue about what needs to be done and what are the interconnected challenges as part of *collective sensemaking*.

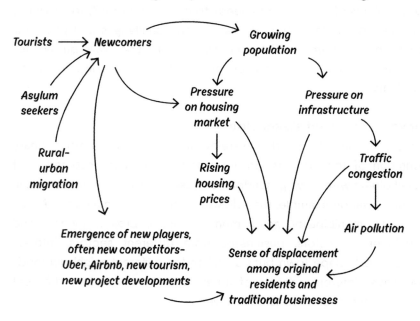

A rich picture is, of course, not a complete representation of reality. Inevitably, systems belong to larger systems and are themselves comprised of several sub-systems. City authorities can look for solutions that transcend their own borders. Amsterdam is doing this in connection with tourism by partnering with NBTC Holland Marketing, with whom it shares the vital strategic goal of distributing tourism more evenly across the Netherlands and across the seasons.[31] There are also sub-systems within the city, each with its own stakeholders and interests groups that are specific to that sub-system. Inviting relevant stakeholders in exploring such sub-systems on the issue of urbanization in Amsterdam, will involve residents specific to those neighbourhoods, project developers investing in that area, existing and new businesses, neighbourhood teams, etc. They can add to the the picture above with their stories and specific situation.

Identifying systems elements and drawing them allows you to visualize a shared story in which the key elements of a complex social problem shows how you can connect those elements to one another. Mapping the complexity makes clear that there are many intervention points/ possibilities but also that any intervention affects all other elements. An explicit story helps in conducting a targeted exploration of the scope, influence and interdependencies of the various elements. This is precisely the point of *collective sensemaking*.

> **Rich pictures make scope, influence and inter-dependencies explicit**

Collective sensemaking can lead to a paradigm shift and the introduction of new simple rules. If all stakeholders in Amsterdam were to realize that opinions on city marketing, such as 'tourists are good for the economy, so the more the better' must become more nuanced, it would be easier to make changes to policy and regulations. When different stakeholders have diverging ideas, *collective sensemaking* can lead to new, more inclusively formulated questions that everyone is interested in discussing.

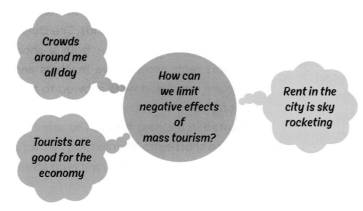

Smart systems interventions

We can focus on *smart interventions* when there are shared perspectives, openness and trust. It also reduces the risk of polarising discussions. When dealing with complex challenges, linear interventions – 'problem X means solution Y' – are not 'smart'. Linear solutions are often sought close to problems and usually seem quite logical: *'if smoking is bad for your health, quit smoking'; 'if you are overweight, eat less'; 'if too many migrants arrive in your country, send them back'.*

Smart systems interventions, by contrast, may be deployed in different places in and around a system. With the example of smoking, for instance, it is possible to intervene at different system levels, such as taxing cigarettes, discounts for non-smokers for health insurance and banning smoking in public spaces.

> **Smart system interventions are 'smart' because they are not obvious**

An important advantage of *systems interventions* is the opportunity to intervene at several places simultaneously. Multiple small interventions that support change in the same direction are preferable to large-scale one-off actions because they cost less, provoke less resistance and are quicker to generate feedback. When interventions in systems are smart, solutions can achieve structural and long-lasting effects on more parts of the system immediately.

To illustrate, at the start of the 2018/19 school year, a huge shortage of primary school teachers became evident in the Netherlands. The Dutch Ministry of Education, Culture and Science opted for both a short and long-term approach. In the short term, prospective teachers and graduates without a degree in primary education were allowed to take on teaching positions. For the long-term, they announced increases in teacher salaries to be implemented in the near future. The effect of salary increase remained unclear. The short-term intervention carried a risk of lowering educational quality, which could on the long term affect the reputation and popularity of the profession.

This problem is not a new one. Salary increases have been lagging for years; retirement numbers have been increasing; and the status of the profession has been declining for some time. Recruitment of new teachers has become an urgent priority. This situation could have been avoided if multiple actions reinforcing chosen policy measures had been taken. It needs to be said that centrally driven policy decisions or monetary solutions may not always be the most powerful intervention. Interventions that affect our biases have a stronger impact. The announcement by Merel van Vroonhoven that she was stepping down from her prestigious top position at the Dutch regulatory body for financial markets, AFM, in favour of a career in special education, was probably more meaningful than a one per cent salary increase.

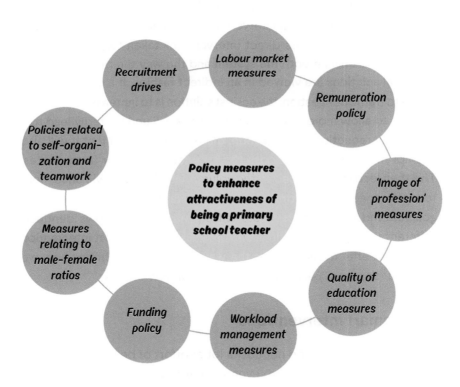

Systems innovation should focus on smart interventions. 'Smart' refers to paying attention to every small step taken to see what follows. Interventions can have unpredictable, even opposite effects that may exacerbate the problem instead of resolving it. To illustrate, in the 1930s, production and consumption of alcohol in the US was banned, a period referred to as the 'prohibition'. This well-intended plan had disastrous consequences: while alcohol consumption initially declined, people soon learned to distil their own. Some of these home-made concoctions were of poor quality, which resulted in health risks and even deaths. Organized crime thrived through the sale of illegal alcohol. The Mafia managed to corrupt members of the police force, making the justice system less reliable. Prohibition also put an end to revenues the U.S. government had been generating through taxes and levies on legally sold alcohol. Lastly, the entire hospitality industry suffered as a result of prohibition. Thousands of jobs across the value chain disappeared: breweries and distilleries, bars and cafes, cask makers, distributors, etc.

Donella Meadows (1999) demonstrated how we can deploy *smart systems interventions*. Her work revealed that the most direct, concrete, visible and straightforward intervention is typically less effective in the long run than several less-direct interventions taken together. Indirect interventions change both the system and the way the problem and its potential solutions are viewed in an indirect fashion. If a certain road is prone to traffic congestion, the easiest solution is to increase the number of lanes to allow more traffic flow. While this will undoubtedly lead to a temporary reduction in congestion, there is a likelihood that it will also prompt more people to choose the broadened road for faster routes. This then leads to increased traffic volume, which in turn, will once more result in congestions. *Smart interventions* entail making explicit what the goals are and afterwards, facilitate self-organization. Meadows identified different systems interventions and indicated that the best intervention is one that effectively changes the way people think. Shifting how we think, our dominant paradigms, is of course, a slow process.

Top 7 smart interventions

Smart interventions need not cost a lot of effort or be expensive to be effective. We have described seven *smart interventions* that could result in *systems innovation*:

1 Acknowledge the complexity
2 Challenge your own thinking
3 Experiment with boundaries, goals and rules of the game
4 Take advantage of accelerators
5 Forge connections

6   Start small and local

7   Give a 'voice' to things that seem negligible

1 Acknowledge the complexity

When we accept complexity as a given, our approach to *wicked problems* changes. It prevents our tendency to break problems down into manageable parts with the aim to find quick solutions. Acknowledging complexity means accepting the uniqueness of each problem and its context; and realizing that 'best practices', successful solutions elsewhere, will not work. It is important therefore to identify all possible aspects or manifestations linked to the problem. *System drawings* are an effective tool for this purpose. Through visualizing the problem and diagramming the relationships between elements, the problem becomes more transparent and more readily understood at a structural level.

Systems drawings help us realize that *wicked problems* straddle areas related to multiple domains and knowledge fields. When dealing with *wicked problems*, the risk of falling into monodisciplinary or specialized problem-solving approaches is limited when stakeholders of all related domains and knowledge fields are present. In acknowledging complexity, different definitions, diagnoses and solution proposals are expected. Usually, those with dissenting viewpoints are often seen as rebellious, negligible, insane or even criminal. However, it is their deviating viewpoints that often contribute to finding solutions; more so than like-minded persons or people in power imposing their views.

2 Challenge your thinking

When we change our thinking, we perceive *wicked problems* differently. A complete shift of a dominant paradigm can change perceptions of a problem and therefore, resulting in novel interventions. An example is of Copernicus, who claimed that the sun, and not the Earth, was the centre around which the planets revolved. This was a shocking contention going against the common worldview of that time.

By thinking differently, it is possible to arrive at surprising new hypotheses and insights, such as: '*prisons breed criminals*'; '*broader and better roads increase traffic accidents*'; '*less regulation of traffic encourages drivers to pay better attention*'; and '*starting small, controllable forest fires prevents widespread blazes*'.

We need to think differently about the future when dealing with *wicked problems*: long-term plans are not effective; traditional solutions of strategic plans with an underlying vision do not work. With *wicked problems*, strategic decision-making should focus on a preliminary course of action and the first next step whilst keeping other options open. The first step is often logical and its consequences manageable. By initiating the first step, we observe how this affects the system as a whole and based on this, decide on what follows: is this the right direction? Or, do we need to adapt our course? Agile methodologies adopted in software development for solving unknown and complex problems, have moved away from blue-print approaches where everything is designed in detail. For *systems innovations*, every change begins with the first next step, and often changing our assumptions is a good place to start.

3 Experiment with boundaries, goals and rules but timing is important

To effectively change our goals, timing is critical. The timing is right for new climate change ambitions due to visible melting of artic icebergs.

The cycle shop, whose slogan is 'experience personal mobility', is branding its product to match the 'experience economy', resonating current trends, and therefore expanding its boundaries of selling just a bicycle.

Changing the rules of the game can be a *smart intervention*. *Catenaccio* football, a defensive style of play with which the Italians achieved great successes in the 1960s and 70s, was copied by other clubs. However, this strategy was abandoned in 1992 when a new rule was introduced: goalkeepers were not allowed to use their hands when returning a ball passed to them by a teammate. Football became more attractive with offence-based styles since returning to the goalkeeper became a risky proposition.

Eliminating existing rules often yields more benefit than introducing new ones. In the Northern Netherlands, experiments with 'shared space'[32] were conducted, in which rules and traffic signs were removed to encourage individual responsibility in traffic. The results have been overwhelmingly positive: the quality of public space has improved and inhabitants have taken initiatives to address bottlenecks. People have become more social in traffic.[33] Local self-organization works well in solving complex challenges.

Experimenting with systems boundaries involves stretching the given space of a system, but also imposing limits on a system: establishing 'caps' on pay checks of CEOs; to growth of companies/countries; exploitation of natural resources, etc.

4 Take advantage of accelerators

Accelerators of *systems innovation* are *attractors*, *drivers of change* and *weak signals*.

When the overall trend (*attractor*) is towards increased sustainability and decreased regulatory pressure, interventions aimed in that same direction will benefit from being carried along by the current.

An example of *drivers of change* is that of social media. They are strong *accelerators* for negative things such as fake news, polarization and manipulation and misuse of personal data; but also, for positive things like access to knowledge, openness, democracy, social justice and cooperation.

Use of social media for positive change can contribute to worldwide paradigm shifts that are needed in the *wicked world*. An example of this is the #MeToo movement against sexual assault and harassment that brought women's rights to the forefront and the need to dispel misuse of power in highly competitive and lucrative industries like the film and broadcasting industries among others, but also in some cultures.

Gretha Thunenberg's protest on Fridays, went viral and contributed to an accelerated shift in giving youth a 'voice' on their future and climate change.

Weak signals, whilst initially unnoticed, often become accelerators: the rise of self-diagnosis and self-medication could seriously change the course of national and private health services systems.

5 Forge connections
By bringing together past, present and future, we can achieve interventions that lead to *systems innovation*. A good example of this is the transformation of abandoned railways into public parks, as was the case of the Promenade Plantée in Paris and the High Line in New York. The High Line was an old, rusty section of raised track from a freight and commercial railway line. For years, the track was abandoned as demolishing was too costly for the city until private owners next to the tracks wanted it demolished to allow expansion of their property or redevelopments. However, private initiatives forged ties with the city and funders to save it. The High Line was redeveloped from 2006 to transform it into an elevated pedestrian boulevard offering scenic views of New York City. The success of the re-design, was also due to the Dutch landscape architect Piet Oudolf who transformed the space to house plants, seating, strolling pedestrians but also signage promoting cultural attractions, shops and restaurants. In 2018, the 'Luchtpark Hofbogen' was opened above the former Hofplein railway station in Rotterdam. Here, once again, an existing structure was used to create something new through connections to new ideas, resources, people, etc., rather than being demolished.

To arrive at *smart interventions*, forging connections is essential: this could be revisiting contacts or creating new ones; connecting products, services, expertise and innovation capacities. Collaborating in networks and clusters is essential for organizations to deal with challenges that cannot be solved alone. Connecting outside the current system often brings greater benefit even as we can make connections within existing systems.

6 Start small and local
Keep interventions small and local for a start. Bring stakeholders together without a previously established plan; keep an open mind and be trusting. Start by working with people who are genuinely eager to help or to solve the issue that is impacting them. By starting small and local, we can experiment at a modest scale and learn what works and what does not. We need to accept that failing is not a bad thing, it is part of the process. Start by trying something different: include other people, other experts; celebrate, maintain and share successes; this is the key to continuously attract new ideas and developments.

In Langa, a township near Cape Town, busses filled with tourists used to drive through the streets to observe life in townships. The people of Langa, however, had no benefit from being a tourist attraction. A ward councillor (a representative of one part of the township) came up with the idea of having walking tours organized by its residents instead. This offered a more direct and authentic experience and led to more contact between residents and tourists. The townspeople also began selling local, traditional arts and crafts to tourists. The programme was a success: a trade school was established to teach locals how to make high-quality products. Police officers and bin collectors returned to the neighbourhood and a recycling company handed out food vouchers to people who collected plastic waste. Langa became an example of local self-organization thanks to a small intervention with major transformative power.

7 Give a 'voice' to things that seem negligible
Watch out for dominant stakeholders and avoid being one yourself. The opinions of dominant stakeholders are often viewed as more important simply because those individuals have power, knowledge or money. When there are dominant voices, other inputs are missing in the search for

solutions to *wicked problems*. Results often are not forthcoming; other stakeholders are disheartened; and eventually they leave. This means that the problem is further from being solved as these stakeholders and their respective informal networks are also lost.

When it comes to *smart interventions*, everyone is important: those who protest; external experts; stakeholders with little influence; and those we perceive as unimportant. All differing perspectives are needed in order to arrive at new types of solutions. Nonconformist thinkers ensure that overused existing strategies that have proven unsuccessful are not deployed repeatedly.

Systems that are governed by a few stakeholders, or have rapid growth based on a dominant, single perspective will develop unilaterally. Such systems are vulnerable. The banking sector where powerful financial interests and singularity of self-growth and prosperity led to the credit and euro crises; and organizations that stress quantitative output measures such as earlier example of hospitals focussed on bed occupancy rates instead of lives saved or made healthier. Often, hard measures are preferred as qualitative measures are difficult to measure. These organizations risk losing their legitimacy in the long-term. The COVID-19 crisis has uncovered the significance of 'vital' services and those who serve in these services, highlighting the imbalance of the economic system that has not rewarded these 'true heroes'. More than 5000 academics across 700 universities signed an op-ed article on the need to re-evaluate shareholder value maximization paradigms and to democratize work and employment (The Guardian, 15 May).

Mobilizing allies for change

Mobilizing *allies* starts with an initial group where mutual trust is established. They share perspectives and awareness of the *wicked problem* and how to move forward. The next step is to expand the circle of allies. *Mobilizing allies* is not about consolidating a power base – it is about finding stakeholders who are prepared to accept the complexity of the issue at hand, and willing to work together in seeking *smart systems interventions* and implementing them.

Four 'levers' that can help in gaining stakeholders' support, are
- timing and rhythm;
- listening and comprehension;
- sense of urgency;
- create clarity.

Timing and rhythm

We described earlier in the book how incidents and crises often present an ideal opportunity to find the allies you need to affect a drastic change or series of changes. These moments act as pivotal intersections. According to Rob Zuijderhoudt (2007), changes that lead to a turning point often display discernible patterns: in complex systems, self-structuring processes that are relatively stable become less stable, these processes move into chaos only to eventually transform into a new and more complex stable order. This process begins at a point when no apparent major issues are at play, even as increasingly, more behaviours or patterns deviating from the existing order emerge. These deviations become amplified and a crisis arises but these fluctuations and deviations continue till it is chaos. During this period of chaos, competing interests clashing with one another form coalitions, ready to fight for their own benefits. In the midst of the chaos, however, a germ of a new order emerges and continues to develop into a new and more complex structure.

Applying proper timing and rhythm means understanding and leveraging processes of complex systems and their characteristic patterns. For example, avoid presenting detailed, fully thought-out ideas for change if no one (as yet) recognizes the necessity for such changes – this is especially true before impending 'chaos' begins. Once there is unrest and signals of complex systems change are noticed by multiple parties and in different areas of the system, it is time to act to form **Activate change allies** coalitions – this is when an existing system becomes destabilised. During the process of coalition building, expanding your circle of allies is more important than persuading your opponents. To gain momentum and impact, focus on finding allies, adding voices and volume to a chorus calling for change is important to create the 'seed' of change of the new order. In Zuijderhout's model, when the chaos grows: proponents and opponents fight with one another and everyone involved loses sight of the finish line. At that point, the greatest chance of success lies with a proposal that offers a path out of the chaos, which will offer relief for both proponents and opponents.

Selecting the right moment for an intervention makes the difference between failure and success. Sometimes it is too early to act, while in other instances, the momentum may have already passed. Bear in mind that dynamic systems have self-regulating mechanisms and therefore, often it is wiser to pause before intervening, than rushing to act.

Listening and comprehension

Proponents and opponents are always right from their point of view. Constantly repeating that 'they' are wrong will not turn opponents into proponents, or vice versa. Instead, listening and understanding why the opponent is 'right' is more useful, explore their perspectives: What is their context and the history? What line of reasoning led to their conclusions? What are they afraid of losing? Asking these questions yield information that is highly useful in seeking *smart interventions*.

We cannot change systems on our own Proponents and opponents are all part of the same system. The only way to resolve complex problems is by involving all stakeholders in the issue. Input from 'opponents' is vital in order to make *systems innovations* effective. When it comes to making changes, only a limited number of people will be fervently in favour or vehemently opposed, while the rest are usually indifferent. This insight can be leveraged for change.

Proponents of change often make the mistake of focusing on those parties who offer the greatest resistance. This requires tremendous energy and only increases the likelihood that viewpoints will harden and polarization will emerge. Seek connections with active proponents and begin experimenting at a small scale. If those experiments are successful, more moderate proponents will become involved, which, in turn, will persuade neutral parties to join your side. By doing so, you gradually work your way towards a paradigm shift.

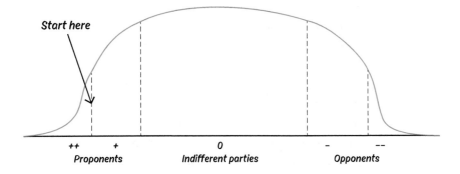

Sense of urgency

Super wicked problems are *wicked problems* whose time is running out, and often the people seeking a solution are also the cause of the problem. In such cases, everyone has ownership of the problem, but no one accepts responsibility: a typical case of politicians sticking their heads in the sand. We previously mentioned greenhouse-gas emissions as an example of a *super wicked problem* that has led to nearly inescapable climate change.

When addressing highly complex problems, we must repress the urge to look for a single comprehensive solution (Levin et al., 2012). A comprehensive solution will never work because it leads to even greater resistance, more acceptable compromises and more attempts to delay and avoid the matter at hand. All of which costs valuable time. The two major challenges in tackling *super wicked problems* are the limited time horizon applied by individuals, businesses and politicians in the search for solutions, and the limited scale at which they are accustomed to examining the effects of their behaviour. Everyone, millions of other people, think that an evening of barbeque or burning wood for warmth in the garden is negligible, but each firewood on a summer evening heats up the earth.

Sense of urgency as a factor promoting *systems innovation* benefits from a combination of solutions. Take, for instance, the following:
- Investing in campaigns to raise awareness and encouraging positive actions aimed at behaviour modification next to enforcement works: in the Netherlands, in fifteen years' time, the 'BOB' campaign against

drunk driving reduced the number of people getting behind the wheel after consuming alcohol by more than half.[34]

- Linking individual behaviour to collective interest: subsidising various energy-conserving measures while simultaneously emphasising the link of such measures for the well-being of future generations; clearly connecting benefits of solving social challenges to sustainable value creation and long-term business practice.

- Looking for local solutions and what makes them unique: the legacy of infrastructure built up over time and unique geographies (city/rural/resource rich, etc.) determine in part which solutions will be most appropriate. This applies to all *wicked problems*, from youth care, unemployment, poverty to mobility, communication, energy and food needs, economic growth. When local solutions succeed, it stimulates others to seek their own unique solutions.

- Recognizing the value of self-organization: this is related to the idea of looking for local solutions; people who organize themselves will be more deeply involved and willing to implement change as opposed to solutions organized 'top-down'; civic initiatives for *systems innovation* are on the rise – safety, healthcare, energy and housing are examples – community-based initiatives make life more meaningful and better while keeping down costs.

Create clarity

People generally dislike uncertainty and ambiguity. The inclination to resist change and keep existing systems is linked to the disposition of avoidance of uncertainty. We need to give clarity in cases where multiple stakeholders in change processes are involved.

Clarity and purpose, and good explanations of intended interventions are necessary, next to processes and roles. There needs to be transparency about who is participating, what the intended results are and what (estimated) costs will be. Next, clearly define each party's role and the expectations of individual contributions. Lastly, provide clarity regarding the structure of how things will be organized and how decisions will be taken.

In conclusion

Systems innovation requires trust, transparency and integrity between the parties involved. *Wicked problems* are persistent and tend to emerge in new forms in different places in the system. *Systems interventions* are needed for structural solutions. *Systems innovation* is the result of creating shared awareness and new perspectives. Nurturing and gaining *allies* instead of focussing on opponents works best. Deploying *smart interventions* as 'levers' for *systems innovation* increases chances of finding answers to complex problems. When it comes to *systems innovation*, the most important advice is: Get started, it does not matter where you start, learn and keep things moving.

4

Policy innovation

The financial and COVID-19 crises have clearly highlighted institutional and systemic failures. Governments have been pressured to deal with complex, persistent challenges with policy suites and instruments that were not designed for such problems. New ways of solving such issues are needed. This search for new approaches in policymaking encroaches all levels – local, regional, national, supranational and global. Understanding complexity and working with new partners is the way forward for governments in search of new roles and shared responsibility, even as we need to recognize that time-tested approaches are not working. How can we accelerate processes of co-creation and collaborations whilst being custodians of just, safe and ordered societies?

Traditional approaches

Governments design their apparatus (agencies, departments, procedures, etc.) to ensure efficiency and transparency for equitable and responsible public services. The scope of public services is extensive and it covers all systems levels. These include, national and domestic security, critical infrastructure, education, health, housing and welfare services, community centres, etc. To offer predictable, reliable and transparent services, laws, rules, regulations and protocols are some of the policy instruments in place. In addition, for every policy domain, specialized departments and services are often created to increase efficiency. Most public services, for legislative and executive tasks, are designed in this way.

We have seen that governments, with their extensively specialized and compartmentalized approaches, are not able to deal with many complex societal problems, such as viral outbreaks, elderly and youth problems, traffic congestion, crime, public disorder, urban migration, energy supply, etc. These departments and processes were not designed to deal with interconnected and multi-domain, multi-system, multi-discipline challenges.

Applying standard responses to complex problems is current practice: establish priorities, create working groups, project groups and, or special programmes, hire external consultants, etc. There is no guarantee such approaches will work because policies are sometimes made without involving key stakeholders: those who are part of the problem, those who may be part of the solution, those who are affected and those who have specialized expertise.

Need for policy innovation

Multiple publications on complex and persistent challenges in the public sector point out the growing demand for policy innovation.[35] In part, due to complex problems, but also due to austerity measures, fragmented government departments are forced to cooperate and seek innovative solutions.

In many countries, the seeds of systems and policy innovations are emerging, some examples are:
- Direct communication between residents and public services via apps allows for faster work processes and results; greater flexibility and efficiency; but also ensures a direct responsibility for the civil servant involved for every action taken or abstained.
- Increasing government support in the Netherlands (and elsewhere) for civic initiatives related to employment, health services, child care, security and maintenance of public spaces in neighbourhoods and villages: citizen groups can apply for funding and other resources to improve their part of the neighbourhood (building playgrounds; increase or improve green landscaping, etc.). Initiatives comes from citizens; and the job is tasked by these civic groups conforming to regulations and public safety standards.
- Inviting start-ups to propose solutions for complex challenges is a trend to break open traditional ways of solving societal challenges: the Start-up in Residence(sTiR) programme was initiated in 2014 in San Francisco that aimed to bring new technologies used by start-ups to work closely with civil servants to deal with challenges related to public safety, housing, earthquake recovery, homeless citizens, foster care, etc. This initiative has taken root in other parts of the world that also tackles issues; and the main spin-off is civic entrepreneurship innovating policy approaches.

Barriers to change

We see that policy innovations are not making headway in the race to address complex societal problems. There are numerous obstacles that hamper change:

- interests, positions, roles and strategies steeped in history;
- power imbalances amongst stakeholders;
- acting and thinking in hierarchies;
- process-driven instead of content-driven;
- focussed on indicators and targets;
- the 'system' hampers solution resolution; .
- working on single systems levels;
- underestimating the power of civil society;
- tendency to ignore nonconformities.

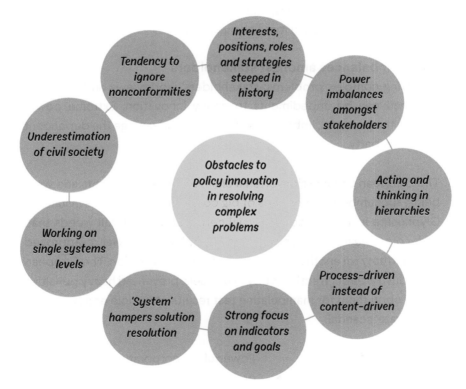

Interests, positions, roles and strategies steeped in history
Historically developed interests, positions, roles, policy strategies and preferred solutions often impede much needed policy innovation.

Civil servants traditionally have power and influence in decisions regarding issue of permits, tenders, designing plans for public spaces, etc. Removing or changing tasks are not always in the interests of those involved, also because of their conviction that (their) expertise is critical for successful policy implementation. Traffic regulators are convinced of the need of traffic lights for citizen safety even as experiments have shown that less regulation in some instances can be more effective.

The dominant animosity between Republicans and Democrats in US has driven proceedings in Congress to a battle of parties instead of serving the public, tackling urgent challenges: health care; decent wages; affordable housing; increasing homeless populations; opioid and other substance abuse; organized and violent crimes; affordable education; systemic and institutional racism in civic and public interactions with black and coloured citizens; immigration challenges; growing disparity between rich and poor; climate change; etc.

Power imbalances amongst stakeholders

In solving complex problems, stakeholders' worldviews and power of influence can be impediments to policy innovation. Extreme power favours the powerful; imbalances of power disadvantage the dependent or weaker party.

The European Commission, often a champion of citizen rights and well-being, succumbed to pressures of big corporations in various instances. Glyphosate is a highly controversial herbicide used to kill weeds that, under pressure from agrochemical company Monsanto, was re-approved for use in 2017 for another five years in the European Union. The European car-industry, through active lobby in Brussels, prevented heavy penalties levied upon them for manipulating test results of vehicle emissions, the 'dieselgate' scandal.

Power is still the greatest determinant of outcomes

Powerful corporations negotiate or coerce national and regional governments and agencies for favourable conditions to locate in their areas. Economically disadvantaged regions are particularly susceptible to accept conditions of such corporations to boost economic activities. The reverse is also true in some cases: a street vendor is no match for municipal authorities.

The Occupy Wall Street movement in New York was a visible protest to the huge power and equity imbalances dominating the US, which also caught on in different parts of the world. The cry for new and more equitable societies were again repeated in more recent protests of the 'yellow vest' and MeToo movements.

In many countries, there was a significant time lapse before it was realized that the coronavirus was killing both residents and staff in nursing and care homes because all the safety measures were aimed at hospitals and their intensive care units. Often, many 'silent' or less visible stakeholders are simply forgotten or discounted in the midst of coercion and pressure of dominant parties when policy decisions are made.

Acting and thinking in hierarchies

In times of crises, centralized decision-making is accepted without resistance in the hope of stability and certainty. We have seen how many leaders embraced the opportunity for a top-down approach to the COVID-19 pandemic threat: China, Russia, Iran, Cambodia, Pakistan and Serbia demonstrated the clearest examples. The approach taken by countries like Taiwan, a number of Scandinavian countries and Germany whereby adequate response and decisive actions to ensure safety first had initially proven to be more effective.

Social welfare work has for a long time and in many places assumed that the 'expert knows best' and treatment plans are designed for the 'clients'. Professionals are in the lead, municipality staff determine the target groups and how money is distributed, police, when involved, follow protocol, etc. The target group - the word choice reflects the hierarchical thinking - have very little to say. Innovative practices that put the person (instead of the 'client') in the lead have reversed social work approaches and power balances within this domain. This approach, also known as Family Group Conferencing, was initiated in New Zealand from Maori traditions and adapted to become Dutch and European movements. It changed the notion of the 'problem' person to understanding that the person is really the start of the solution.[37]

Process-driven instead of content-driven

We have seen a shift from 'led by experts' to 'managers of processes' in many areas of policy, particularly in the Dutch context. Often, domain experts have been replaced by process managers in governments, hospitals, education, healthcare, social work, etc. These process-driven managers are focussed on optimizing operations to achieve targets in a systematic, planned manner based on time-tested methods. Standardized protocols and methods are not focussed on the broader contexts or interdependencies of a problem when attempting to find a solution. The dominance of business efficiency in policy areas is not useful in tackling *wicked problems*.

Process-oriented managers and those responsible for the 'content'

Managers: Process-driven	Domain experts: Content-driven
Sensitive to intricate nature of problems, with an inclination to break them down into sub-problems before each part is solved separately.	Sensitive to complexity of issues, with an inclination to include the broader context when addressing such problems.
There is no tolerance for errors in meeting business targets: efficient planning and monitoring controls help solve any issues immediately. Process efficiency is key.	Solutions need to be anchored in the 'content' (subject matter) of complex, interconnected problems pertaining to individuals and groups. People and subject-matter are key.
Budgetary constraints, target performance contracts, resource capacities utilization and other quantitative output data leading in managing issues.	Finding smart, efficient and sustainable approaches to tackle issues.
Guided by categorization, operational processes, standard formats, protocols, projects, procedures and rules.	Interdisciplinary dialogue and cooperation with everyone involved; experimentation to find the best possible approach.
Approach anchored in uniformity and standardisation in dealing with issues.	Approach anchored in acknowledging unique and context-specific nature of issues.

Focussed on indicators and targets

When we use targets to monitor our progress, the risk of adjusting goals to measurable and easily attainable goals is present. Daniel Kim (1997) refers to this common phenomenon as 'drifting goals'. The risk of *drifting goals* is quite high when dealing with *wicked problems*.

Prisons, for example, choose to focus on cell occupancy numbers rather than the person locked-up. Similarly, hospitals shift to 100% bed occupancy goals instead of the people occupying beds.

When municipalities adopt 'the number of inhabitants served' as a performance indicator as opposed to measuring their success by how effectively each person is helped, they aggravate complex issues in the constituency. When the emphasis is placed on numbers, employees tend to help 'easy' customers first to raise their performance score, whilst more 'difficult' customers with complex cases are left for later. On the surface, a municipality appears to be operating successfully. However, in reality, the number of severely neglected cases is growing, and no attention to effective prevention policy is developed because the problems remain invisible until it is too late.

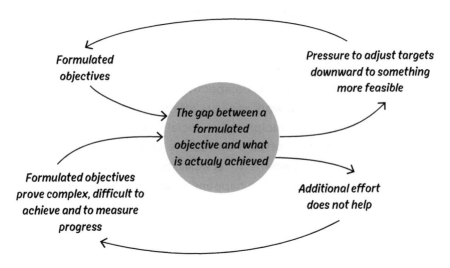

Adapted from: Daniel Kim, *Drifting goals* (1997)

The 'system' hampers solution resolution
'Systems' are often built around the people running the system rather than around the clients, customers or consumers.

The main issue with innovating 'systems' is that the people who administer and safeguard a given system are also the ones who are expected to change it (OECD report).[36] This is not easy since government bodies are organized on the basis of services and departments, mandates and domains. For instance, the social domain of government is distinct from the work & income domain: each has different legislative foundations; each has its own professional jargon; policymakers and civil servants in each domain possess different expertise; and the working methods and procedures are also different. However, citizens do not have 'domains'; when someone loses his or her job, they may need welfare and other 'social' services until they find new employment. From a citizen's perspective, integrating social and economic domains makes more sense.

Gatekeepers are 'bad' systems innovators

Working on single systems levels

Complex problems act on multiple systems levels simultaneously. We have shown through examples earlier on how *systems innovation* can be realized when proper consideration is paid to the interactions between systems and the various system levels.

In many municipalities, the focus on providing individual assistance hampers a more sociological perspective on social care issues: How do individualized social work services affect those needing help and those providing it? Are recipients of social work services becoming dependent on the care offered due to the customized approach of social work; referral systems to specialists; extensive waiting lists and current regulations? What happens to social workers when their mandate and continued employment is dependent on policy priorities and projects that use performance targets and output figures based on personal scores? Such approaches do not support development of prevention programmes and effective interventions for issues that transcend individual care issues. When focussing on social services provisions to individuals, no attention is given to broader themes like social inequality. Solving structural challenges of equal opportunities, regardless of gender, race, class age, etc., require interventions not as individuals but at other system levels.

Daniel Kim (1997) calls this systemic phenomenon 'fixes that fail': solutions that keep the systemic problem in place. *Quick fixes*, designed for single systems level, are addictive and hard to avoid as they are temporary successes that feed the need to resolve issues.

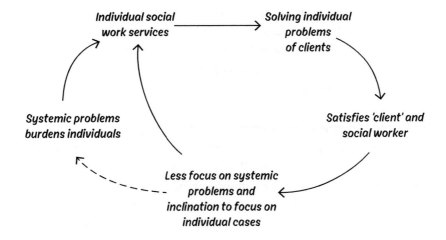

Individual social work services → Solving individual problems of clients

Systemic problems burdens individuals

Satisfies 'client' and social worker

Less focus on systemic problems and inclination to focus on individual cases

Adapted from: Daniel Kim, *Fixes that fail* (1997)

Underestimating the power of civil society

The established order, including governments, are often taken by surprise when civil society, deeply dissatisfied or angry, become a force to be reckoned with. People and institutions of power became complacent in their positions of influence and take their assumed *carte blanche* positions for granted. They become myopic; ignore or underestimate simmering shifts in moods and other developments in society. To illustrate, developments that were initially underestimated, specifically in the Netherlands but also elsewhere, are protests against wind turbines,[38] resistance to vaccines,[39] the rise of populist political movements,[40] the discussion surrounding the Dutch Zwarte Piet,[41] the impact of gas extraction on surface ground[42] and increased earthquakes[43] (parallels protests to fracking) and the resistance to CO_2 storage.[44]

Greta Thunberg, the Swedish climate activist, was initially not taken seriously as she independently organized student strikes for accelerating the climate change agenda. Her single voice and actions were amplified through social media, TED talks, climate change conferences, marches against climate change and global school strikes. These events got her an audiences with the European Commission, the World Economic Forum, the United Nations, the European parliament and the Vatican.

In nearly all cases, initial reactions of the established order are to marginalize such issues, including initial societal responses. This changes when bottom-up and external forces gain critical mass and cannot be ignored. This leads to policy makers and those who stagnated change to re-assess their standpoint.

Tendency to ignore nonconformities

The final obstacle in the way of policy innovation are ignoring deviating or non-conforming behaviours. Policymakers often are slow to establish timely and essential contact with newcomers, unconventional thinkers, critics, criminals, and other marginalized groups. There is a tendency to ignore non-conforming behaviours and those who do not fit the 'norm', even when policy is about them. Involving stakeholders in policymaking could lead to innovation that is inclusive and aligned to their circumstances.

Prompt responses to new developments are difficult when interventions will bring about (major) changes to existing situations and interactions. Employment shortages and related labour market challenges in health care and education sectors have continued to persist, as well as dealing with impacts of tourism locally, drug- crimes, disoriented persons, cybercrime and air transport.

Complex problems often arise gradually. Initially, there is only a *weak signal* that hardly anyone notices. Gradually, this changes: first the problem is noticed locally by a few people and minor interventions are administered; at this stage, no one perceives the latent scope or magnitude of the problem yet; next, the problem severely impacts larger groups of people, who increasingly demand solutions to the problem; it is at this stage that the problem becomes a 'policy issue'.

New approach

Given that barriers to change exist, how can a new approach be realized to tackle complex societal challenges? How can policy innovation be achieved? Recommendations for policy innovation have parallels to those for *systems innovation*. What follows are recommendations specific to *wicked problems* in society that demand policy changes.

These include the following:
- map the complexity;
- make the 'issue' leading;
- align policy direction at all system levels;
- redistribute knowledge, power and control;
- make use of transformative powers;
- incorporate co-creation practices;
- be alert to differences: power, interests and (non)participation;
- integrate policy innovation into 'the system'.

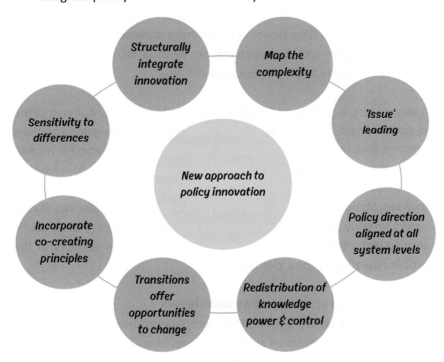

Map the complexity

As with *systems innovation*, complex issues of social policy cannot be resolved by breaking them down into smaller problems and assigning these sub-problems to different departments and services. Quick solutions at a single level within a single system will often backfire. Complex policy issues call for a thorough diagnosis of the problem at hand and an effective analysis of the aspects involved.

Identify aspects of the situation:
- Explore the broader landscape in which the problem exists, the history of the problem, the internal and external influences at play, the various stakeholders and their interests and differing perspectives on the problem at hand.

- Investigate how the problem relates to other problems and other systems.
- Be alert to crises, dilemmas, paradoxes and escalations.
- Look for opportunities to connect to the self-correcting and self-organizing ability of involved parties and the systems in which they operate.

Make the 'issue' leading
Every *wicked problem* is different. We need to allow the 'issue' at hand to determine who (internally and externally) needs to be involved in developing new policy directions. Different stakeholders can provide different insights and perspectives on '*what is making the problem worse and what is helping to mitigate it?*'

Stakeholders, including policymakers and civil servants, are all part of the system related to a problem. Their involvement in designing solutions ensures that their role in stagnating, improving or worsening a *wicked problem* is made explicit. When the 'issue' (*wicked problem)* is leading, the unique circumstances of the problem determine how to move forward. Standard protocol does not work – local circumstances always vary. Currently, problems are identified and delegated to related public service departments or policymakers who then tackle aspects of the problem related to 'their' domain.

Align policy direction at all system levels
Designing clear policy direction for complex problems is important to ensure that all actions taken at all policy levels are aligned. We have seen how countries and governments are organized into policy areas and domains, departments and services, etc., to ensure specialization and efficiency. This highly specialized way of working has created 'silos' or islands, each with its own interventions.

Performance indicators impede *systems innovation*

To mitigate climate change, different measures are taken by different countries, regional governments and local municipalities. These measures across all systems levels need to be aligned. Not by a centralized detailed plan, but having overarching policy direction. Reducing climate change to 2 degrees of the 1990 benchmark by 2030 was an overarching goal.

Countries then designed policy directions such as increasing x% of current renewal energy of energy mix; or reducing CO_2 emissions by x% within 10 years; or all policy targets need to be tested for contributions to climate change targets, etc.

Designing broad policy directions offers alignment whilst giving room for interventions to meet specific local contexts. Having varied but complementary interventions are more effective than a single massive action.

Policy alignment for *wicked problems* often need to include global pacts: UN Sustainable Development Goals, Treaty on the Non-Proliferation of Nuclear Weapons (also known as the Non-Proliferation Treaty), Paris Agreement on Climate Change are some examples of setting global policy directions.

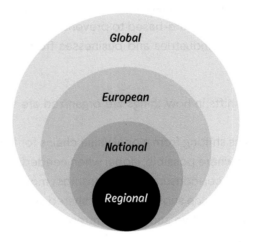

Redistribute knowledge, power and control

Revisiting current positions, roles, procedures, working methods and expertise is an important first step in developing new policy approaches to complex challenges. Breaking open current practice, could allow alternative and unconventional views of new stakeholders to participate in seeking new pathways. Room for new experiments lead to different answers to complex questions. The start-up in residents programme is one such example that originated in San Francisco.[45] This successful programme has been replicated in many cities elsewhere and has accelerated policy innovation.

Policy innovation calls for a redistribution of power and re-thinking existing roles taken by governments, even as coordination is needed since more and new parties will be included in solving complex challenges. By relinquishing some or all of its conventional role as custodian of public good, governments still retain their authority, and may in fact gain trust

New roles for governments

by doing so. Measurements of policy should no longer be directed to controlling precise outcomes but about coordinating policy direction by setting framework conditions, inclusion of stakeholder engagement and participation and creating productive collaborative processes.

Make use of transformative powers
We can make use of the transformative power of transitions.[46] Transitions are on-going in various domains:
- in energy: from fossil-based to more sustainable sources;
- in health care: from cure-based to prevention, cure when needed;
- digitalization of industries and businesses from analogue systems; etc.

But also, major shifts in how things are organized are seen in examples such as:
- supply chains shifting from global value chains for low costs to local value chains where possible, global when needed;
- shifting producer-consumer relationships moving from product ownership to service subscriptions or shared systems;
- increasing cooperative and social entrepreneurships connecting to the 'purpose' economy where societal challenges are driving these shifts.

Policy can connect to such new movements and those exploring alternative ways to solve societal challenges since governments cannot solve societal problems alone. It remains logical that governments should coordinate all initiatives and collaborations aimed to solve societal challenges given their responsibility to safeguard public interests.

We often see that various initiatives are taken to solve social challenges but many such problems keep coming back as *wicked problems* are persistent; continue to negatively impact many people; and no one knows what to do next. Governments, in that case, must act:

- initiate, frame the 'challenge' and create framework conditions;
- connect to those experimenting in related transitions and orchestrate the process;
- participate in the search for systemic solutions;
- commit and co-fund developments.

Collaborators in transition experiments often include those from academia, civic organizations, businesses and citizens. New forms of cluster collaborations aimed at societal challenges such as to clean oceans, energy, healthy aging, water management, biodiversity balances, etc. reflect 'quadruple-helix' partnerships to accelerate transitions.

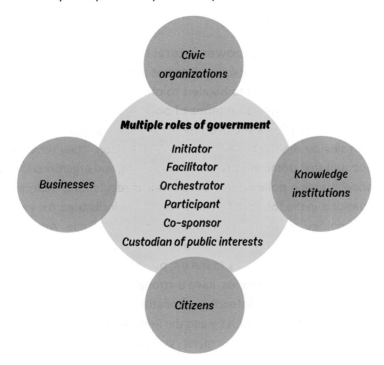

Incorporate co-creation practices

A combination that has proven both productive and innovative in dealing with complex issues is intensive partnerships between policy institutes, residents, businesses, knowledge institutions, non-governmental organizations (NGOs[47]) and financial institutions. This has been demonstrated in the Silicon Valley economic cluster but also recently, in fighting COVID-19. Co-creation and co-designing are at the core of such approaches. Complex problems that seem impossible to resolve need to make use of co-creation and co-design principles.

'Wisdom of the crowds' is a term used to capture the availability of knowledge and insights everywhere. In traditional approaches, experts and specialists had all the answers and this holds true to date for specialized fields that can solve very complicated problems. However, with *wicked problems* and *systems innovations,* everyone involved is needed and has answers to different parts of the puzzle. For policy development, solutions can emerge from direct consultations of citizens of specific demographic groups, residents, 'clients' or consumers.

When co-creation and public consultations in policy interventions are applied, the chances of successful systems and policy innovations are considerably improved.

Be alert to differences: power, interests and (non)participation
In dealing with *wicked problems*, different groups need to be included. In this, governments need to be alert to differences that exist between various stakeholder groups in terms of power, viewpoints, interests and the capacity to participate. Governments, as they are legitimately placed in their roles by their voters, have a strong position. They have to take into account that dominant players have a strong and organized lobby to influence strategic policy decisions as well as regulations. Multinational corporations, in the tobacco, automotive and oil industries, for example, and technology and digital platform giants like Google, Amazon and Apple have more prospects to influence policy than small and medium sized businesses and citizens. In the US, party lines, connected to strong industrial and political lobbies, have a strong influence on how policies are shaped. The 'right to defend' as a constitutional right has seen strong connections to the arms industry and the Republican party, which in turn, make policy innovations surrounding gun violence in the US difficult to address in the given political landscape.

 Power invokes short-sightedness

There are always strong advocates in dealing with *wicked problems* and policymakers need to heed disparities in power, interests, presence or absence of different voices in shaping policy. Often, stakeholders are forgotten or neglected.

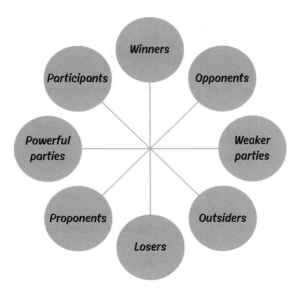

Including all types of stakeholders is vital in finding effective solutions; seeking out
- people with deviating opinions;
- those who are not in the forefront of societal discussions;
- 'losers' of potential solutions;
- proponents and opponents of potential solutions;
- ways to generally lower participation thresholds.

Integrate policy innovation into 'the system'

Innovation cannot be delegated to project and programme modes as and when a need arises to solve new problems; *ad hoc* approaches will not lead to sustained policy innovation cultures. Therefore, continuous efforts aimed at behavioural change and developing a culture of innovation is needed.

Governments are expected to be predictable, reliable and transparent. At the same time, they must respond to incidents, both minor and major, and to emerging societal issues whereby no set rules or procedures are in place. This requires government systems to span two distinct types of activities demanding different types of capacities and competencies.

Two distinct systems with opposing qualities

System 1	System 2
Hierarchical and administrative	Flexible and improvising
Diligence and accuracy	Quick response in crises
Focus on stability and predictability	Dealing with insecurities
Standardized procedures	Creative solutions
Equal treatment	Room for customized treatment
Control and monitoring	Room for experimenting and by trial and error
Focus on services	Focus on stakeholders

Traditionally, the first system is well-anchored in government organizations. The second system and the necessary competences are becoming increasingly more important. Often, the latter competences are lacking and temporary measures are taken by creating think tanks, steering committees, project and programmes that transcend individual services or departments of government agencies. The *ad hoc* and temporary nature of such groups do not help change institutional culture as mentioned earlier. Both systems and their respective competences are needed in governmental organizations.

❛ New competencies needed for systems innovation

With 'standard' situations, existing protocols are adequate; with 'complicated' situations, suitable specialists are able to resolve the problem; with 'complex' problems, competences identified in '*System 2*' are needed. Engaging with stakeholders (inside and outside departments and government bodies) to map the complex situation and work towards effective interventions are key to resolving complex situations.

Weick and Sutcliffe (2011) talk about 'mindfulness' in their book *Managing the Unexpected: Resilient Performance in an Age of Uncertainty.*

How is behavioural change achieved? They emphasized the importance of organizations able to cope with unexpected situations. They stressed the need to stimulate shifts in organizational culture across the board.

Their recommendations included:
- Focus on monitoring small failures – do not be blinded by successes.
- Avoid oversimplifying events and situations – you may lose important details.
- Focus on operations - *what is happening on the ground*.
- Focus on resilience – adapt constantly to new situations.
- Value expertise wherever you find it – usually, the experts are not at the top.

Weick and Sutcliffe show how behavioural changes achieve changes in organizational culture, and not the other way around.

Wicked problems and global policy innovation

Global challenges are of such proportions that any proposed plan of action will inevitably fall short of tackling them. Climate change and the COVID-19 pandemic have shown how difficult it is to coordinate these complex challenges. Complexity approaches can offer support to such challenges when it comes to global policy developments. We will explore the COVID-19 pandemic, a phenomenon that is still unfolding, to present a cautious first attempt to illustrate this.

In mapping the complexity of the problem, the systems drawing reveals how policy was reactive at various levels on discovery of the viral outbreak. To instil pro-active policymaking changes in the future, there needs to be changes in perceptions and responses at different levels of policy, and this will take time.

The COVID-19 crisis of 2020 emerged so quickly that there was simply no time to think about *systems innovation*. Governments the world over had no choice but to take emergency measures, namely, breaking up the physical spread of the virus meant immediate 'lockdown'.

The COVID-19 crisis, in turn, generated new crises around the world: in healthcare, in education, in cultural and social aspects, and the economy. Growing complexity was evident at every systemic level. Across the globe, across Europe, in every country, region and family contexts. Complex problems are characterised by uncertainty regarding which interventions will prove effective.

Given the unpredictable nature of complex problems, uncertainty reigned over the effectiveness of any intervention. All nations experimented with policy measures to combat the virus. Everywhere interventions were copied from other regions and results were monitored. Dilemmas arose as to which problems were most urgent and increasingly more people and professionals got involved. Once the medical urgency and contagion control measures were in place, a new and urgent dilemma arose: when can the lockdown and other restrictions be reversed? How do you do this and when? The economy, social and mental health issues were taking their toll and the dilemmas became more pressing with time. The most important lesson from the crises was that there was no shared vision or a long-term strategy in place to prevent and manage pandemics, even as scientists have been warning of such events.

The complexity of the COVID-19 crisis

In an article in the *New York Times Magazine*, 'How Scientists Could Stop the Next Pandemic Before It Starts' of April 21, 2020, Jennifer Kahn describes how scientists have long been convinced that local virus outbreaks could potentially lead to a global pandemic. Steps needed to be put in place to handle the predicted pandemics. In order to achieve this, they knew that this is only possible if powerful parties dedicated themselves to preventing such disasters.

Kahn explains why governments, pharmaceutical companies and the WHO failed to do so. The chief reason being that it was unclear when an actual threat would emerge – it could have been another 30 years' time before it presented itself:

- Governments, faced with austerity and other challenges, were wary of spending enormous amounts of money needed on prevention measures.

- Pharmaceutical companies were reluctant to invest in broad-spectrum vaccines against viruses because they had no idea when they could recoup their costs.
- The World Health Organization lacked the necessary resources and power even though they had the mandate to take leadership in this.

The systems diagram reflects the resulting complexity and how authorities at all levels acted in a reactive fashion; and not everyone activated restrictive measures immediately – only after the virus arrived and began to wreak havoc in their region did the authorities enact measures.

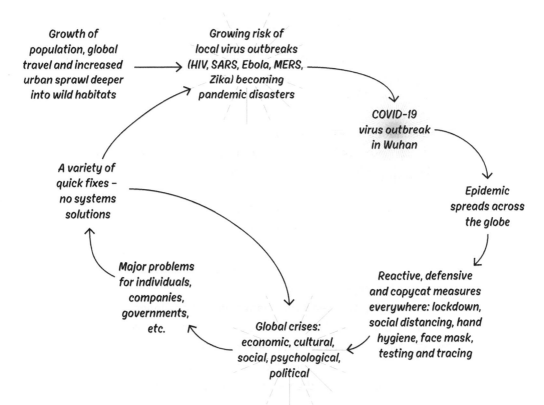

Reactive policy measures prioritizing short-term interests are also evident in other complex problems like climate change and urgent environmental issues. Here too, divisive interests of countries, political leadership, businesses with their shareholders stand in the way of realizing long-term strategies and *systems innovation*.

There needs to be a coordinated and mandated global approach to resolve global challenges that could reduce impacts of future life-threatening pandemics. A mandated global authority could, for instance, initiate, orchestrate and facilitate collaborations in the search for broad-spectrum vaccines, identify high-risk viruses, monitor disease hotspots, take measures to reduce risks of viruses passing from animals to humans and, if needed, lockdown measures whereby such regions would be self-sufficient.

The way forward – what can be done differently?

The task is not an easy one but the depth and scope of crises facing global communities may help speed up awareness and action towards policy innovation at the global level.

Recommendations for a global approach includes:
- **Need to acknowledge gravity and interconnected global challenges:** various complex issues affecting the global community could ultimately pose a threat to our continued existence. Examples include climate change, the risk of pandemics, population growth, environmental pollution, secure and affordable food, energy supplies and reliable global infrastructures. These issues do not stand alone, they reinforce one another and therefore necessitate general guidelines for long-term policy at a global level.
- **Acknowledging the need for change:** global challenges cannot be solved in isolation as they are connected to other *wicked problems*. Policymaking needs to consider how to restructure the way we have organized our world to diminish or even eliminate such problems.
- **Review dominant paradigms:** it is possible to consider such a restructuring of the world only when we are prepared to critically examine today's dominant paradigms. Competition, profit in the short term and the growth of individuals, companies and countries are currently viewed as much more important than future generations' chances of survival. It is precisely those survival odds for humanity that must be embedded in the core of both long-term policy and the underlying paradigm.

- **Need for global mandate**: visions for the future are present on every continent and in every country. However, a global approach is missing. An initiative such as the UN's Sustainable Developmental Goals needs to be endorsed and the UN or some global agency needs to have the mandate to enforce general principles agreed upon in close collaborations with all nations, supported by expertise and funding to this end.
- **Connecting macro, meso and micro-levels**: room for ideas, initiatives, approaches to thrive at all systems level, global, national, regional and local. This allows for a rich pallet of diverse approaches and solutions. Whilst at the global level, general principles and policy directions are agreed upon, bottom-up initiatives can bring about new impulses for change.
- **Strengthen local communities and regions**: more attention is needed to make communities and regions self reliant, less vulnerable and more resilient. New technologies can facilitate local self-sufficiency.

Strengthening regions

Globalization fuelled the growth of regions like London and Silicon Valley, resulting in unprecedented flows of capital, talent and businesses, whilst other regions lost their industries and jobs in part due to global supply chains profiting from cheaper labour and production costs elsewhere. The disparity between capitals/major urban centres and peripheral and rural areas is common in many countries and continents. In Europe, low growth regions of Greece, Italy, Spain and Portugal are in stark contrast to North Western Europe with their metropolitan hot spots feeding off global market growth.

In addition, the COVID-19 pandemic has also revealed and exacerbated deeper structural deficiencies and weaknesses of social and economic inequalities between population groups within and across regions and nations. These developments have seen increased disorder and resistance as described earlier. Systems identities are fraught with conflicting values and interests.

Systemic failures to draw 'lagging' regions but also vulnerable populations into prosperity has seen policy interventions and bottom-up developments to address such disparities.

Silicon Valley spurred many a government to create their own 'success valleys' which, although not always successful, have contributed to the recognition of the value of clusters as a means to coordinate and support innovation, productivity and new business development. In Europe, regional Smart Specialization Strategies frame regional developments with cluster policy not only as an additional tool to accelerate chosen pathways (new value chains, international collaborations, lifelong learning, shared resources, knowledge and goals, etc.) but also to create new interactions and patterns of collaborations and to engage new stakeholders in regional innovation and developments.

Building new ecosystems of knowledge and innovation to improve social, ecological and economic wellbeing is a direction that many regions are taking. This connects to higher systems goals such as the European Green Deal, the United Nations' Sustainable Development Goals, the global Climate Agreement, etc. This shift also resonates with developments initiated by citizens and local communities, but also with a new breed of entrepreneurs and community leaders.

New cooperatives are established by communities or place-based businesses intending to boost and realign economic activities to make local and regional areas more self-sufficient. Building resilience is often at the core of such activities. Place-based cooperatives are taking root in many regions building on older practices of 'The Commons' and collective practices. Preston (UK), Mondragon (Spain) and Westerkwartier (Netherlands) are examples of such place-based cooperative practices that are serving businesses, enhancing social well-being and preserving natural landscapes - with well-being at the heart of their missions. These bottom-up initiatives include governments, educational institutions, businesses and civil society (the 'quadruple-helix') working towards common societal gains; acting as 'social cluster' model movements.

In addition, parallel developments are taking place in the virtual space to boost economic and social activities through Platform Cooperatives that are new avenues for strengthening regional innovation and well-being.

In conclusion

Increasingly, policymaking institutions are taking steps to deal with complex societal challenges. There is also a growing realization that governments have to deal with barriers and obstacles in their organizations that hamper their ability to effectively address complex problems. Policy innovation needs to help governmental bodies to recognize growing societal complexities; ensure power imbalances are addressed and opens up to include others to resolve pertinent challenges; take on orchestrating and facilitating roles; and invest in behavioural changes and organizational culture. These are building blocks for effectively addressing *wicked problems*. Cooperation between parties at the local, regional, continental and global levels are prerequisites for success.

5

Who is in charge?

Legitimacy of traditional leaderships is challenged in a *Wicked World*. Traditional leaders are often not the first to notice the need for change or the first to identify new directions. New ideas, solutions and initiatives can emerge from anywhere. We need to make space for everyone inside and outside the organization to address, voice and work on *wicked problems.* What does complexity leadership look like? What has changed in the nature and scope of leadership? Who is in charge? How do we need to act?

Leading in complexity

I n a dynamic world, 'leadership' takes on an entirely new meaning (Brown, 2011). Leaders are constantly challenged in a continuously changing landscape: the 'rules of the game' and 'who is in the game' are frequently changing. We cannot predict the future; we find it impossible to design long-term strategies in many areas.

We are constantly learning about leading in complex contexts. The following scholars have contributed important insights into the dynamics of complexity leadership.

Myths about leaders

Plowman and Duchon (2008) describe four myths connected to leadership.

Myth 1: Leaders are visionary – create and realize visions for the future due to their ability to understand what is happening around them and mitigate any barriers that may hinder plans.
On the contrary, managers are no better equipped than others in the organization about the occurrences inside and outside the organization. Valuing employees for their inputs throughout the organization leads to productive futures in organizations.

Myth 2: Leaders can manage change.
However, change pops up everywhere, with its own escalating dynamics that runs its own course. Change is all too often unpredictable and

unavoidable. Leading is about discovering underlying patterns in small changes that improve the organization's ability to deal with complex problems.

Myth 3: Leaders provide clarity, stability and order within the organization whilst effectively bridging the gap between goals and results.
On the contrary: [in a *wicked world*] creating discomfort is needed. Prevailing order and stability need to make room for new behaviour to ensure continued survival of the organization and its systems.

Myth 4: Leaders can steer others in a desired direction.
However, 'the desired direction' is never entirely clear as it is never only 'the leader' determining 'the direction'. Leaders should facilitate processes that support emergence of a new order.

Generative leadership
Jeffrey Goldstein, James Hazy and Benyamin Lichtenstein (2010) state that heroic or charismatic leaders tend to mistakenly think that they can single-handedly solve their organization's problems. Leadership is a process: leaders are in networks and interactions confronted by new perspectives and insights, which in turn leads to renewal, flexibility and growth. The authors refer to this as 'generative leadership' that is dynamic and co-evolves with changing environments over time.

One particular phenomenon that they address is laissez faire developments of bottom-up self-organization that result in a morass of unintended outcomes. They advise combining top-down and bottom-up influences to co-exist side by side: leaders should construct 'ecologies of innovation'.

The expanding role of leaders
In their work, Matthew Gitsham and Jo Wackrill (2012) demonstrate how the roles and scope of leaders are changing. Businesses are discovering opportunities to create value whilst serving the larger community by addressing societal challenges and making social or ecological contributions. Leaders in politics, businesses and civil society are increasingly entering into partnerships.

This development changes the leadership role: leaders lead changes that transcend the boundaries of their own organizations. Such a role involves participating in public discourse, proactively influencing behaviours of customers and suppliers, lobbying for changes in industry standards and government policy. Leaders are active in their region and work together with local groups, communities and stakeholders with very different perspectives.

Three types of leadership

Mary Uhl-Bien, Russ Marion and Bill McKelvey (2007) distinguish between administrative, adaptive and enabling leadership.

1   **Administrative leadership** refers to traditional roles of managers focussed on planning and coordination of tasks that is carried out top-down.
2   **Adaptive leadership** takes place in the context of interactive change processes. This type of leadership emerges from conflicting interactions, needs, ideas and preferences, and leads to actions, networks, new technologies and collective response.
3   **Enabling leadership** forges connections between the opposing administrative and adaptive leadership types, and creates favourable conditions for adaptive leadership to allow room for emergent developments such as new interactions, complex networks and systems alignment.

Three key roles of leaders

Edwin E. Olson and Glenda Eoyang (2001) describe three key roles for leaders in complexity:

1   **Defining the organization and its boundary**: *Who are we? What are our objectives? What is our relationship to our environment?* This must be limited to only what is essential and guide people and the organization towards the desired direction and vital outcomes but leave details of work processes to those involved. Distribution of power and creating a *sense of urgency* are both important: leaders should allow space for experiments but also take it back when needed.
2   **Dealing with differences**: different perspectives, opposing views and conflicts need to be dealt with. At the same time, leaders need to nurture diversity as it is an asset in dealing with changes, however slight, in the external environment.
3   Leaders need to **stimulate transformative exchanges** through interactions: encouraging feedback, promoting lateral connections by developing networks of customers, suppliers, government agencies and other individuals and groups who can offer added value.

Shifts in the leadership *bubble*

Changing landscapes of our *wicked world* are re-shaping the leadership *bubble*. Power *bubbles* are being challenged, from within and outside such systems; changing landscapes infiltrate our organizational *bubbles* – leaders have to cope with expanded and more complex playing fields; and these in turn, are bursting traditional leadership *bubbles* – everyone is in-charge, when it makes sense for them to act.

Span of control: power and influence

Upholding positions of power wielding huge spans of control is easiest in isolated systems or *bubble worlds*. Dictators get away with this by isolating their countries from the rest of the world; abuse of power takes place in closed systems and where imbalances of power are present also in other systems like religious institutions, cults and sects, sweatshops, organizations and households with migrant labour where law enforcement is weak, in marriages, etc. Influences from the outside are crucial to exert pressure on dominant and unjust hierarchical power when dealing with 'rogue' nations; whilst law enforcement or punitive measures are applicable for blatant abuses by individuals and organizations.

 A *wicked world* calls for shared power

There is also another trend when it comes to opposing vested power positions and dominant spans of control. Growing groups of stakeholders are increasingly contesting the legitimacy of those in power and competing for a share of such powers.

1   In the geo-political arena, dominant nations are contested for their assumed supremacy: Asia and Asia-Pacific alliances to counter western world dominance in the last century; and recently, in a turnaround of events, US protests of China's span of influence and domination in global trade.

2   Global leaders are wary of global giants in the technology sector like Google and Facebook who have more influence and money than most nations.

3   Cultural and ethnic suppression or injustice fed by notions of supremacy are being challenged by demographic groups in movements like *Black Lives Matter*, but also activist NGOS like *Avaaz* with a membership of 60 million across the globe, coercing those in power to act by organizing petitions, campaigns, protests and supporting local actions to combat indigenous, ethnic, cultural, faith and gender related injustice and oppression.

4   Employees, traditionally organized through labour unions, are joined by customers, supply chain stakeholders, governments, NGOS and public debate, to change practices of extreme imbalances of profit distribution in businesses. Bonuses for the top and disproportionate dividends whilst firing employees and receiving state aid in times of deep economic crises are some topics that are being influenced by those outside the system.

The dominance of western superiority exists only in the minds of some people – some of whom feel victimised by shifting power relationships and act on their fear of being left behind.

We see an erosion of centralized power domination at all levels. At the micro-level, fathers' position as 'head of the household' is diminishing or non-existent in western societies but also, parents feel increasingly powerless in bringing up their children, in part due their inability to deal with complex worlds (Manickam & Van Berkel, 2006).

The *playing field*

The goal of management teams in businesses or institutions is to maintain or expand their own organization. There has been increasingly a shift in organizations paying attention to external developments seeping into their establishments. Managers are no longer limited to their own organizations only – their playing field has been altered. Focus has shifted to the organization as a system that exists amongst other, continuously innovating systems. This also holds true for those in the profit, public and the third (charities, NGOs, etc.) sectors. The rise of the Internet has changed communication and competition worldwide, even as other developments have empowered and fuelled socially driven individuals, organizations and coalitions, leading to blurring traditional consumer-producer/client-specialist/citizen-civil servant roles and, giving rise to new economic, business and public service models.

❛ The playing field is larger than any individual company

The 'playing field' for all leaders has expanded, become more diffuse and is volatile, and this, demands constant and greater attention. These include developments such as:

- new and advanced technologies coming from all corners of the world;
- massive amounts of knowledge existing elsewhere;
- businesses and higher education institutions joining forces, in existing or new clusters and value chains;
- the circular economy as a pivot to ensure ecological and socio-economic sustainability on the long run;
- sharing economic models with their cooperative principles leading innovation, production, distribution and consumption of goods and services;
- the supra-national blocs creating new boundaries for common markets to enable free movement of goods, services, capital and people to varying degrees across different regions in the world: European Union, Southern Common Market (Southern America trade bloc) Association of Southeast Asian Nations, Common Market for Eastern and Southern Africa, North America Free Trade Agreement, Asia-Pacific Economic Cooperation, Greater Arab Free Trade Area, Australia New Zealand Common Economic Region Trade Agreement, The Pacific Alliance, etc.

'Old' context

- Internal aspects: shareholders, hierarchy, operational processes, output
- External aspects: competitors, customers, suppliers, statutory frameworks

'New' context

- Collaborating in networks with other businesses, consumers, citizens, government agencies and knowledge institutions
- Growing societal themes: mobility, ecological sustainability, climate change, shared responsiblity, social media, etc.
- Global competition and communications

Leaders and the changing playing field

⟶

Just as organizations are faced with enlarged and more diffused playing fields, the world has gotten 'bigger' and more complex for all of us, also at the individual level. Young people are growing up in a world of possibilities and options, rather than a world of certainties. They can no longer count on a steady job with a fixed income with a smooth career path. Instead, they have to take charge of their livelihood and upkeep themselves.

Who is in charge?

I magine that a group of people are given, in pairs, a rope that they have to hold at the ends. Next they are asked to create a massive knot in the middle. A manager is then assigned the task of disentangling the 'knot' by directing the group from a distance. Each time the manager gives an instruction, the entire 'system' changes. People wait to be told what to do, not much happens and the process takes too long and the participants start to get bored. Untangling the knot seems an impossible task for the manager.

Now imagine that the participants are instructed to untangle the 'knot' on their own: what follows is a swift process where they are taking initiatives, seeing effects of their actions – whether the knot is getting bigger or smaller – deciding if they need to act, or wait for their turn, moving as a group to solve the problem. The system acts and behaves differently than previously. Every participant is alert and involved, and the knot is disentangled in a fraction of the time it would have taken with a manager in charge.

Efforts to tackle *wicked problems* will invariably involve many different parties, each with their own perspective on how to improve an existing situation. Traditional leadership roles prove to be counter-productive as shown in the 'knot' example, when it comes to complex problems. It is extremely difficult to work effectively when working requires attention to multi and different perspectives.

Dijkstra and Feld (2011) explain that shared leadership is a way to rid ourselves of current systems of centralized organization and leadership. Every individual in an organization has specific knowledge and skills;

everyone has a responsibility related to their role and function to do what needs to be done; and everybody can take the initiative. Everyone is expected to respond to others and to cooperate, and each party takes independent decisions with regard to their own sphere of influence. In addition, all parties are required to learn, further develop their talents, keep abreast of current developments and learn how to do things better. In short: everyone takes the lead, when it makes sense.

> **❛ Everyone is in charge: when it makes sense, take the lead…**

The trend is clearly visible, initiatives abound in the shape of bottom-up self-organization, more so than in the past. In businesses, employees take on community services or do crowdfunding for charities to create better connections with their local communities; during the COVID-19 crises, businesses, organizations and individuals took initiatives from making face masks, offering transport and child care services to those in essential services, particularly in the health care; many artists offered free concerts from their living rooms or for the elderly isolated in nursing homes; teachers created on-line activities and learning materials for children to maintain their development before formal digital lessons started up, etc.

This trend was already visible before the COVID-19 crisis, in the personal lives of many individuals. Social services have been cut in many welfare states. The elderly for example, must take care of their future – there is no certainty about who will nurse them when the need arises – even in societies that traditionally cared for the elderly in extended family structures, whilst in many European nations, residential or nursing care homes are becoming scarce or too expensive due to budget cuts.

Systems innovation: attitude, demeanour and behaviour

No one person alone can truly grasp complex situations. Everyone has their own expertise, span of influence, specific interests and biased perspectives. This is why cooperation is fundamental to *systems innovation*. When we take the lead in our *wicked world*, we need to deal with diversity on many levels and this demands behaviours, attitudes and demeanour from all involved.

Competences for systems innovation

The *systems analysis and systems innovation* frameworks, integrated in the drawing below, show the interconnected nature of being in, understanding and dealing with complex adaptive systems.

We have learnt how we need to acknowledge and accept *systems dynamics*; conflicting and divisive interests as critical aspects to embrace and use; of the significance of communication patterns and interactions; and the presence of power differences. Tying this together is *systems identity*. These insights help us design and effectuate *systems innovation* through connecting, experimenting and mobilizing stakeholders from within and outside the systems.

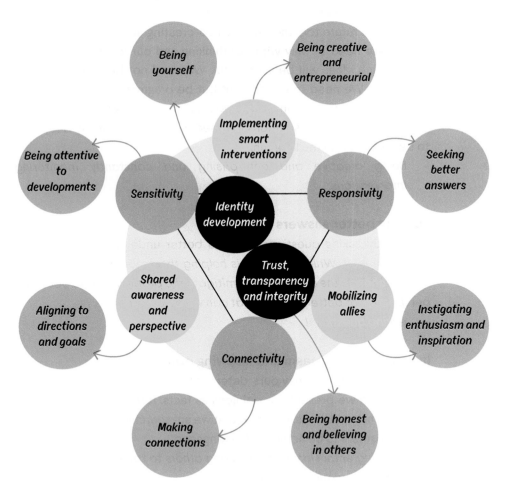

Systems innovation competences are connected to our own personal identity development and abilities to connect and create new interactions, dialogues and actions across differences spanning multiple systems and system levels.

Being yourself

Knowing who we are will enable us to be seen by others. This includes our history and experiences, of crises and successes, and of our knowledge and competencies. In order to present ourselves, we need to know our strengths and shortcomings, dilemmas and certainties, expectations and interests, values and norms, goals, loyalties and worldview.

– *'Being yourself' is being honest and open in working with others.*

Being creative and entrepreneurial

Designing a future together involves co-creating and co-designing with others. We need to play with our thinking and our ideas as we do not know which ideas will be successful. We need not be afraid of wrong outcomes. We need to experiment but be pragmatic in our approach. We must be on top of things – be alert and adapt quickly when things do not work. Sometimes, solutions may seem successful initially but prove to be disastrous in the long run.

– *Being creative and enterprising and constantly monitoring interventions.*

Seeking better answers

Constantly asking questions to get a better understanding is part of taking the lead: *Which situation is helping the problem escalate? How can we change the ecosystem to mitigate the problem and to get some perspective of better times? What can we do better?*

– *Asking questions!*

Instigating enthusiasm and inspiring others

Our attitudes and behaviours determine how others respond to our input. When we present our opinions as facts, it makes others passive. When we ask questions, we show that we are searching for answers. This prompts others to be active and be engaged.

– *Creating enthusiasm and inspiring others to take action and share their own unique contributions.*

Being honest and believing in others

Being honest, *'say what you think and do what you say'*, is also about being reliable and transparent. Self-reflection is important: *why we think, say and do things? And how do these choices affect others?* Believing in others is not about carte blanche positivity of the qualities and intentions of others but it is about our own judgements and implicit biases. Positive judgements are a good basis for cooperation. Negative judgements, perhaps based on first impressions, lead to frustration and stagnation for all sides.

- *Seeking the strength and transformative power of all individuals is at the core of believing in others.*

Making connections

Connecting to new themes that transcend our professional discipline and familiar arenas; and connecting to others who can contribute to solving the issue. Professionals are efficient within their respective areas of specialization as they are experts in their fields. However, there are downsides to this. Routines and familiarity create professional distance: a doctor grows accustomed to sickness and death whilst a civil servant relates to migrants as numbers and quotas rather than recognizing personal histories and identities. The nature of *wicked problems* demands that professionals look beyond their normal boundaries. Engaging with those who hold different views and diverging opinions and sharing with them problem definitions and solutions can help with finding new ideas.

- *Making connections requires pushing beyond our limited boundaries to ignite new perspectives and create solutions.*

Aligning to directions and goals

Aligning with others who have different perspectives requires resolve. *How does the other party interpret the situation? What analyses are plausible? What do we agree on and where do our opinions differ? Can we agree to a new and shared definition of the problem, so that new paths and goals can take shape? What difference can we make together?*

- *Willing to cooperate requires designing new and shared definitions and interventions together.*

Being attentive to developments and playing our parts

When we are sensitive to what is taking place around us, we can contribute to resolving the complex challenge. We need to be able to see and feel what is going on, and sense when something is wrong. Keeping focussed on developments outside the system is important and asking ourselves how can we contribute constantly is key. *What can we do? What is our added value? What can we contribute to improve the situation, and what can we do to stay relevant as that situation develops?*

–   *Being attentive to outside developments includes reflecting on how we can help.*

Value driven futures

An unpredictable future does not mean that we are not *in charge*.

We have explored how our thinking, through *bubbles*, *paradigms* and *perceptions*, guides us towards our goals, shaping our actions and the resulting outcomes. Our decisions and actions, like our thinking, are *value driven*. As individuals, but also collectively, our actions and choices create future worlds driven by underlying values. The current *wicked world* is also a result of past worldviews and actions. This includes increasing societal challenges and related systemic inequalities between races, sexes and the haves and have-nots – a web of multiple systemic problems.

We allowed it to happen:
–   our focus on short-term benefits has thrown climate systems into disarray with disastrous ecological consequences;
–   thinking in superiority and inferiority terms has resulted in unequal opportunities for individuals based on gender, ethnicity, religion, sexual orientation, economic position, etc., and ultimately to systemic inequality;
–   inequalities have become anchored in all societal systems: education, the labour market, politics, religious institutions, enforcers of social stability such as police and army, etc.

Systemic inequality is difficult to change – systems reinforce values of the majority or the vested order; equal opportunities are automatically realized if the values promote equal opportunities.

This is why the onus is on us: *we are in charge*. We need to determine our desired future together – *collective sensemaking* as a starting point, driven by new values: *Do we want to end the ecological disarray? Do we aspire towards a circular economy? Do we want to stop systemic racism and sexism?* We need to stop our indifference and act on these new values.

In conclusion

Everyone is *in charge*. Shared leadership is needed in a *wicked world* as everything is interrelated with everything else and the world has become so complex that no one person can oversee the full picture. To play our part in complex challenges, we need attitudes, behaviours and demeanours that promote honest and adaptive interactions, enthusiasm and inspiration in co-creative collaborations. By being aware of what is happening and seeking connection with others, it is possible to find answers to complex questions that will ultimately lead to better *systems innovation*. We need to have *value driven systems innovations* that bring a fair and sustainable world for all.

6

Moving forward...

We live in a *wicked world*, a world affected by complex societal challenges and *wicked problems* for which we have no ready answers. In any case, no straightforward solutions to be designed by any one person or entity – complex problems demand another approach. Insights drawn from systems theory and complexity science can help us with *systems innovation* and policy innovation. Acknowledging complexity and navigating between micro and macro levels where *wicked problems* occur are foundations for initiating *systems interventions*.

Systems and complexity-related theories take into account manifestations of chaos, complexity, 'the unexpected' and 'chance'. These theories acknowledge the complexity of problems; the possibility of unintended escalations arising from interventions; and the unpredictable impacts of other systems and systems levels. Systems and complexity-related theories focus on local situations and on the subjective realities of multiple stakeholders. They show that changes are continuous and give rise to new circumstances in which no single entity has decision-making authority or overview. When we take into consideration these realities in *systems analysis*, we gain different insights and new perspectives for dealing with complex societal challenges and *wicked problems*.

Systems innovation begins with a *systems analysis* to determine which systems features, both inside and outside, contribute to the growth of *wicked problems*. We have outlined four systems qualities for the analysis. The following applies to all systems:

- **Identity**: How does the system define itself and how do stakeholders see the system? What is the history of this system? Which rules govern the system? What is the *path dependency* of the system and what can lead to *path creation*?
- **Sensitivity**: How sensitive is the system to internal and external *systems dynamics*? Which *drivers of change* and *attractors* are specific to this system? Which *weak signals* are we missing?
- **Responsivity**: How does the system respond to developments and interventions, and is this adequate? How *resilient* is it? Can the system co-evolve with its changing landscape? What are '*differences that*

make the difference' in this system and are we using them? Do we facilitate *self-organizing* capacities and movements?

- **Connectivity**: How is the system connected to other systems, networks and themes? Is the system able to connect with other systemic levels? How are *transforming interactions* are taking place and where? What else is needed to make 'the system' relevant and sustainable?

Systems innovation entails the deployment of *smart interventions*, the creation of shared awareness and perspective, and the mobilization of allies. Without openness and mutual trust, it is difficult to find common ground and develop a shared vision of what is going on and needed. *Collective sensemaking* is a heightened process of understanding what is taking place. Dealing with *wicked problems* require insights from different sides, including those we do not agree with. Acknowledge differences; make use of them; and be surprised with what emerges – friction can turn dullness to a glow.

Smart interventions are 'smart' not because they are the most obvious solutions but because they are creative and a result of co-creation and co-design. *Smart interventions* are not huge or exciting. On the contrary, they are often, small and subtle, which makes monitoring and evaluating possible. We can explore what impacts interventions are having on 'the system' and other related systems; and whether developments are moving in the chosen direction.

We tend to challenge changes made by our opponents, which is not useful in tackling *wicked problems*. Instead, we need to mobilize allies who are moderately positive or neutral with regard to the issues we want to address; to identify pivots or leverage points to do this with a feeling for timing and cadence; to listen attentively to neutral groups and opponents; and to de-polarize, create a *sense of urgency* and provide clarity and certainty wherever possible.

Policy innovation is urgently needed with the increasingly daunting challenges facing societies. This can only happen when 'policy' and governments open up; and invite stakeholders, including those 'forgotten', to find answers to these complex challenges.

Policy innovation is a significant form of *systems innovation*:

- Policy can give 'voice' to those left out of important dialogues shaping our futures.
- Policy systems have a greater span of influence and can impact several systems and systems simultaneously.
- Policy innovation can result in new rules of play; change playing fields to offer more equitable and sustainable societies; ensure that *super wicked problems* are given the attention and resources needed.

It needs to be said that it is important not to fall into a common policy (and management) pitfall of seeking consensus resulting in watered down compromises. Dutch culture includes the so-called 'polder model', which served well in conflicting and divisive times, but the unfortunate results were compromises that satisfied nobody.

Systems innovation leans on everyone taking their cue and acting when appropriate. It involves taking charge by making ourselves party to the situation; understanding that we are all part of such systems; by being honest, open and transparent; by forging connections with others; by instilling enthusiasm and inspiration in others; by listening to and stimulating their creativity; and by sharing their unique expertise.

This world is a *wicked world*, which forces us to step off the beaten path and to redesign our worlds. It offers us an opportunity to redistribute power and influence, to develop new ways of thinking and acting, and to establish new connections with one another.

References

Ackoff, R.L. and Emery, F.E. (2017). On purposeful systems: *An Interdisciplinary Analysis of Individual and Social Behaviour as a System of Purposeful Events.* New York: Routledge.

Arum, S. van & Enden, T. van den (2018). Sociale (wijk)teams opnieuw uitgelicht: Derde landelijke peiling onder gemeenten 2017. Movisie. Retrieved from www.movisie.nl/sites/movisie.nl/files/publication-attachment/Sociale-wijkteams-opnieuw-uitgelicht-2018%20%5BMOV-13719898-1.2%5D.pdf.

Balanyá, B. & Sabido, P. (2017, October). The Great Gas Lock-in, Industry lobbying behind the EU push for new gas infrastructure. *Corporate Europe Observatory.* Retrieved from corporateeurope.org/sites/default/files/the_great_gas_lock_in_english_.pdf.

Bateson, G. (1972). Steps to an ecology of Mind. Chicago: The University of Chicago Press. p. 452.

Béné, C., Godfrey-Wood, R., Newsham, A. & Davies, M. (2012). Resilience: New Utopia or New Tyranny? Reflection about the Potentials and Limits of the Concept of Resilience in Relation to Vulnerability-Reduction Programmes. *Institute for Development Studies*, Working Paper 405.

Boersma, H. & Lohman, J. (2018, August 17). 'Weg met het hokjesdenken in de landbouw'. De Volkskrant. Retrieved from www.volkskrant.nl/columns-opinie/weg-met-het-hokjesdenken-in-de-landbouw.

Bos, M. van den (2017, February 6). Wat zijn de basics van het factchecken? Stimuleringsfonds voor de Journalistiek. Retrieved from www.svdj.nl/ nieuws/wat-zijn-de-basics-van-het-factchecken

Bouma, K. (2018, August 10). Tony Wheeler over het 'Lonely Planet-effect': 'Het heeft even geduurd voor we doorkregen hoeveel invloed we hadden' Interview Tony Wheeler. *De Volkskrant*. Retrieved from www.volkskrant.nl/mensen/ tony-wheeler-over-het-lonely-planet-effect-het-heeft-even-geduurd-voor-we-doorkregen-hoeveel-invloed-we-hadden.

Brink, G. van den (2017). Moderne liefdadigheid. Wetenschappelijke Raad voor het Regeringsbeleid (WRR), Working paper 25, p.79-82. Retrieved from www. cbf.nl/Uploaded_files/Zelf/wrr-g-van-den-brink-moderne-liefdadigheid-2017.b40f98.pdf.

Bristow, G. and Healy, A. (2015). Crisis response, choice and resilience: insights from complexity thinking. *Cambridge Journal of Regions, Economy and Society*, 8(2), 241–256.

Brown, Barrett C. (2011). Complexity Leadership: An Overview and Key Limitations. *Integral Leadership Review, October, Learner Papers.* Retrieved from integralleadershipreview.com/3962-learner-paper-complexity-leadership.

Bruce, P. (2017, March 2). When the Big Lies Meets Big Data, *Scientific American*. Retrieved from blogs.scientificamerican.com/guest-blog/ when-the-big-lie-meets-big-data.

Bruijn, H de (2016). *Framing, over de macht van taal in de politiek*, 6de editie. Amsterdam: Atlas Contact.

Chua, A. (2018). *Political tribes: Group Instinct and the Fate of Nations.* New York: Penguin Random House.

Delgado, M., Porter, M. E. & Stern, S. (2014). Clusters, Convergence, and Economic Performance. *Research Policy*, 43, 1785-1799.

Dijkstra, J. & Feld, P-P. (2011). *Gedeeld leiderschap: Veerkracht door nieuwe vormen van samenwerken, organiseren, leren en leiderschap*. Assen: Van Gorcum.

Ehrlich, P.R., Raven, P.H. (1964). Butterflies and plants: a study in coevolution. *Evolution* 18: 568–608. DOI: 10.2307/2406212

Etzkowitz, H. & Leydesdorff, L. (2000). The dynamics of innovation: from National Systems and 'Mode 2' to a Triple Helix of university–industry–government relations. *Research Policy*, 29, 109–123.

European Union (2018). A multi-dimensional approach to disinformation: Report of the independent High level Group on fake news and online disinformation. DOI: 10.2759/739290.

Genus, L. van, Juez-Larré, J. & Jong, S. de (2017). Nederland in Transitie: Van Exporteur naar Importeur, De verander(en)de rol van aardgas in Nederland. (2017). Whitepaper TNO in samenwerking met The Hague Centre for Strategic Studies. Retrieved from www.tno.nl/nl/over-tno/nieuws/2017/8/ nederland-sneller-van-exporteur-naar-importeur-van-gas/

Gitsham, M. & Wackrill, J. (2012). *Leadership in a Rapidly Changing World: How business leaders are reframing success*. Ashridge Business School & International Business Leaders Forum. Retrieved from www.unprme.org/ resource-docs/LeadershipinaRapidlyChangingWorld

Goldstein, J. A., Hazy, K.K. & Silberstang, J. (eds). (2009). *Complexity Science & Social Entrepreneurship: Adding Social Value through Systems Thinking*. Litchfield Park: ISCE Publishing.

Goldstein, J., K. Hazy, J.K. & Lichtenstein, B.B. (2010). *Complexity and the Nexus of Leadership: Leveraging Nonlinear Science to Create Ecologies of Innovation*. New York: Palgrave Macmillan.

Harvey, J.B. (1974). The Abilene paradox: the management of agreement. *Organizational Dynamics* (3), 63-80.

Heylighen, F. (2009). *Complexity and Self-organization*. In Bates, M. J. & Maack, M.N. (eds). (2009). *Encyclopedia of Library and Information Sciences*. Boca Raton: CRC Press.

Holland, J.H. (1992). Studying complex adaptive systems. *Daedalus*, 121(1), 17-30.

Hosmer, L. T. (1995). Trust: The Connecting Link Between Organizational Theory and Philosophical Ethics. *The Academy of Management Review*, 20(2), p. 379 – 403. DOI: 10.2307/258851

Hurst, A. (2018). *The Purpose Economy*. Seattle: Imperative.

Huxham, C. & Vangen, S. (2005). *Managing to Collaborate, the theory and practice of collaborative advantage*. Oxon: Routledge.

Kim, D. (1992). Systems Archetypes 1: *Diagnosing Systemic Issues and Designing High-Level Interventions*. Cambridge: Pegasus Publishing.

Kim, D. & Lannon, C.P. (1997). *Applying Systems Archetypes*. Cambridge: Pegasus Publishing.

Kotter, J.P. (2018). *8 steps to accelerate change*. Retrieved from www.kotterinc.com/ wp-content/uploads/background-photos/8-Steps-for-Accelerating-Change-eBook.pdf.

Kotter, J.P. (2012). Accelerate, How the Most Innovative Companies Capitalize on Today´s Rapid-Fire Strategic Challenges – and still make their numbers. *Harvard Business Review*. Retrieved from hbr.org/2012/11/accelerate

Levin, K. Cashore, B., Bernstein, S. & Auld, G. (2012). Overcoming the tragedy of super wicked problems: constraining our future selves to ameliorate global climate change. *Policy Sciences*, 45(2), 123-152. DOI: 10.1007/s11077-012-9151-0.

Lewin, K. (1947). Frontiers in Group Dynamics: Concept, Method and Reality in Social Science; Social Equilibria and Social Change. *Human Relations*, 1(1), 5–41.

Lünnemann, K., Goderie, M. & Tierolf, B. (2010). *Geweld in afhankelijkheidsrelaties: Ontwikkelingen in vraag naar en aanbod van hulp en opvang*. Utrecht: Verwey-Jonker Instituut. Onderzoek in opdracht van het ministerie van WVS.

Manickam, A. & Berkel, K. van (2006). *Wordt er nog opgevoed? Who is bringing up the child?* Assen: Enova Emancipatiebureau.

Manickam, A. (2018). *Future of Cluster Developments – Lessons from Energy Valley, The Netherlands*. Groningen: Marion van Os Centre for Entrepreneurship, Hanze University of Applied Sciences Groningen.

Meadows, D. (1999). *Leverage Points: Places to Intervene in a System*. Hartland: The Sustainability Institute.

Meeus, J. & Schravesande, F. (2018). 'Narcostaat' Nederland groeit bijna ongehinderd. NRC. Retrieved, 23 February 2018, from www.nrc.nl/nieuws/2018/02/23/narcostaat-nederland-groeit-bijna-ongehinderd-a1593444

Merali, Y. & Allen, P. (2011). Complexity and Systems Thinking. In Peter Allen, Steve Maguire and Bill McKelvey (Eds.). *The Sage Handbook of Complexity and Management* (pp. 31-52). Cheltenham: Edward Elgar Publishing.

Olson, E.E. & Eoyang, G. H. (2001). *Facilitating Organization Change, Lessons from Complexity Science*. San Francisco: Jossey-Bass.

Pariser, E. (2011). *The Filter Bubble: What The Internet Is Hiding From You*. New York: Penguin Press.

Plowman, D.A. & Duchon, D. (2008). Dispelling the myths about leadership: From cybernetics to emergence, in Uhl-Bien, M. & Marion, R. (eds.) *Complexity Leadership: Part I: Conceptual foundations*, 129-153. Charlotte: Information Age.

Porter, M. E. & Kramer, M. R. (2011). Creating Shared Value, How to reinvent capitalism – and unleash a wave of innovation and growth. *Harvard Business Review*, 89(1-2), 62-77.

Porter, M. E. (2003). The Economic Performance of Regions. *Regional Studies*, 37, p.562.

Raworth, K. (2017). *Doughnut Economics: seven ways to think like a 21st century economist*. London: Cornerstone.

Reynolds, C. W. (1987). Flocks, Herds and Schools: A Distributed Behavioral Model. *ACM SIGGRAPH Computer Graphics*, 21(4), 25–34.

Rittel, H. & Webber M. (1973). Dilemmas in a General Theory of Planning, *Policy Sciences*, 4, 155-169.

Shepherd, S. & Kay, A. C. (2012). On the Perpetuation of Ignorance: System Dependence, System Justification, and the Motivated Avoidance of Sociopolitical Information, *Journal of Personality and Social Psychology*, 102(2), 264–280.

Snowden, D.J. & Boone M.E. (2007). A Leader's Framework for Decision-Making. *Harvard Business Review*.

Sull, D. & Eisenhardt, E.M. (2015). *Simple Rules: How to Thrive in a Complex World*. New York: Houghton Mifflin Harcourt.

Sull, D.N. & Wang, Y. (2005, June 6). 'The Three Windows of Opportunity'. *Working Knowledge*. Harvard Business School. Retrieved from hbswk.hbs.edu/archive/4835.html

Sutcliffe, K.M. (2017). Leading with Resilience in the Face of the Unexpected. Leading in Trying Times Essays (2017). *Center for Positive Organizations*. Retrieved from positiveorgs.bus.umich.edu/wp-content/uploads/Leading-With-Resilience-Sutcliff.pdf

Uhl-Bien, M., Marion, R. & McKelvey, B. (2007). Complexity Leadership Theory: Shifting leadership from the industrial age to the knowledge era. *The Leadership Quarterly*, 6(2), 654-676.

Verhaeghe, P. (2018). 'Hoe deze maatschappij eenzame individuen creëert'. Retrieved from www.human.nl/lees/2018/Hoe-deze-samenleving-eenzame- individuen-cre-ert-.html

Weick, K. (1993). The collapse of sensemaking in organizations: The Mann Gulch disaster. *Administrative Science Quarterly*, 3, 628–652.

Weick, K. (1995). *Sensemaking in Organisations*. London: Sage.

Weick, K. (2001). *Making Sense of the Organization*. Malden: Blackwell Publishing.

Weick, K.E. & Sutcliffe, K.M. (2007). *Managing the Unexpected, Resilient Performance in an Age of Uncertainty* (2nd ed). San Francisco: Jossey-Bass.

Weick, K.E. & Sutcliffe, K.M. (2011). *Management van het Onverwachte, wat je kunt leren van High Reliability Organizations*. Amersfoort: BBNC.

Zuijderhoudt, R. (2007). *Op zoek naar synergie - Omgaan met onoplosbare problemen*. Universiteit van Amsterdam. Retrieved from hdl.handle.net/11245/1.310708

Index

Notes

1   A study conducted by the Utrecht Data School, which analysed all Twitter activity from a two-week period in 2016, showed that the group of political Twitter users consists of two clusters: one leaning to the left and one leaning to the right. These groups make very different choices regarding the type of messages they share with their respective networks. Source: nos.nl/nieuwsuur/artikel/2213563-schaduw-macht-twitter-als-politieke-machine

2   'But facts are, as we know from cognition psychology, not facts for the brain – they are informations without meaning until they become 'framed' by emotion and belief.' Tristan & Horx, M. (2017, November 10). Source: http://www.gap-minder.org/news/working-with-enlightened-cognitive-dissonance/

3   'Post-Truth' was chosen as Oxford English Dictionary's Word of the Year for 2016, because it was used so often during the Brexit referendum and during the American presidential elections in that year. Oxford English Dictionary. (2016). Word of the Year 2016. Source: en.oxforddictionaries.com/word-of-the-year-2016/

4   Groupthink is 'a mode of thinking that people engage in when they are deeply involved in a cohesive in-group, when the members' strivings for unanimity override their motivation to realistically appraise alternative courses of action.' Janis, I. (1972). Victims of groupthink: a psychological study of foreign-policy decisions and fiascos. Boston: Houghton Mifflin Co.

5   Authors: K. Dooley (1996). 'A nominal definition of Complex Adaptive Systems, The Chaos Network', p. 8. P. Cilliers (1998). Complexity and Post-modernism: understanding Complex Systems. S. Chan (2001). Complex Adaptive Systems: Research seminar in Engineering Systems. R. Axelrod & M. Cohen (2001). Harnessing Complexity. Basic Books.

6   The components of a complex system that interact with one another referred to as 'agents'. These may be people or termites or countries or drones or businesses within an economic cluster. We will use the word 'stakeholders'

7   Retrieved from http://www.cbs.nl/nl-nl/maatwerk/2018/17/regionale-economische-groei-2017

8   Retrieved from: https://www.cbs.nl/nl-nl/nieuws/2016/37/pbl-cbs-prognose-groei-steden-zet-door

9   'The Cluster Emergence Model' from Manickam, A. (2018). 'Future of Cluster Developments – Lessons from Energy Valley, The Netherlands'. Groningen: Marion van Os Centre for Entrepreneurship, Hanze University of Applied Sciences Groningen.

10   Foresight Future Identities (2013), Final Project Report. The Government Office for Science, London, p.9.

11   'Drifting Goals' from Kim, D. (1992). Systems Archetypes 1: Diagnosing Systemic Issues and Designing High-Level Interventions. Cambridge: Pegasus Publishing.

12   De Nederlandse politiebond [The Dutch Police Union]. (2018, February). 'Noodkreet Recherche: Waar blijft onze versterking? [Detectives sound the alarm: where are the reinforcements we need?] Source: www.politiebond.nl/ actueel/nieuws-and- blog/noodkreet-recherche-waar-blijft-onze-versterking

13   Retrieved from https://www.fastcompany.com/26455/next-time-what-say-we-boil-consultant

14   Retrieved from: https://pdfs.semanticscholar.org/3087/ addf40b7ed3215423ca6286f0c4c0a7cad23.pdf

15   Retrieved from: https://www.siliconvalleycf.org/sites/default/files/ publications/svlg-report.pdf

16   Retrieved from http://ditissauwerd.nl/wp-content/uploads/2018/07/Dorpsplan-Sauwerd-en-Wetsinge.pdf

17   McKinsley Global Institute (2017). Jobs lost, jobs gained: What the future of work will mean for jobs, skills, and wages. Source: www.mckinsey.com/fe- atured-insights/future-of-work/jobs-lost-jobs-gained-what-the-future-of-work- will-mean-for-jobs-skills-and-wages

18   https://www.weforum.org/agenda/2018/01/how-to-make-artificial-intelligence-inclusive/

19   Meaningful differences in a system such as power, level of expertise, quality, costs, gender, race and previous education can lead to the emergence of patterns in that system. Adapted from: Olson E.E. & Eoyang G.H. (2001). *Facilitating organization change: lessons from complexity science*. San Francisco: Jossey Bass, p. 13.

20   Edward Lorenz posited described how a butterfly flapping its wings could set off a chain reaction that, several weeks later, causes a tornado in an entirely different location. Predictability: Does the Flap of a Butterfly's wings in Brazil Set Off a Tornado in Texas? Lorenz, E.N. (1972, December 29). American Association for the Advancement of Science, 139th Meeting. Original article: Lorenz, E. N. (1963). Deterministic Nonperiodic Flow. Journal of Atmospheric Science, 20(2), 131–140.

21   https://theguardian.com/sustainable-business/2016/jul/04/gurgaon-life-city-built-private-companies-india-intel-google

22   'Health cuts most likely cause of major rise in mortality, study claims' from The Guardian (2017, February). Consulted from www.theguardian.com/society/2017/ feb/17/health-cuts-most-likely-cause-major-rise-mortality-study-claims

23   From questions to opportunities, 25 routes, namely: The blue route: water as a path to innovation and sustainable growth; Building blocks of matter and the fundamentals of space and time; Circular economy and efficient use of resources; sustainable circular impact; Sustainable production of healthy and safe food; Energy transition; Health research, prevention and treatment; Young people in development, parenting and education; Art: research and innovation in the 21st century; Quality of the environment; Living history; Logistics and transport in an energetic, innovative and sustainable society; Materials – Made in Holland. Measuring and detecting: everything, always and everywhere. NeuroLabNL: the top practical lab for brain, cognition and behavioural research; The origin of life on Earth and in the universe; Towards resilient societies; Personalised medicine: the individual as the starting point; The quantum/nano-revolution; Regenerative medicine: a game changer headed for broad application; Smart industry; Smart, liveable cities; Sports and exercise; Sustainable Development Goals for inclusive global development; Between conflict and cooperation; Creating value through responsible access to and use of Big Data; Consulted from wetenschapsagenda.nl/routes/

24   A fantastic metaphor found in 'How trees secretly talk to each other' from BBC News. Consulted from www.youtube.com/watch?v=ywoqeyPIVRo&feature=youtu.be

25   Taken from newspaper articles in the Volkskrant (April 14) and NRC (4 July 4) 2017.

26 'Hoe werd het Koninklijke Philips groot? [How did Royal Philips become so successful?]' by Lent, N. (n.d.). Consulted from npofocus.nl/artikel/7495/hoe-werd-het-koninklijke-philips-groot and 'De verlichte onderneming Stork: Geen strijd maar samenwerking [Stork, the enlightened enterprise: cooperation rather than conflict]'. Lak, M. (2007). Historisch Nieuwsblad, 8. Retrieved from www.historischnieuwsblad.nl/nl/artikel/6978/de-verlichte-onderneming-stork

27 https://www.un.org/sustainabledevelopment/sustainable-development-goals/

28 Consulted from: www.forbes.com/sites/neilwinton/2017/09/26/dyson-british-vacuum-cleaner-plans-electric-car-assault-with-2-7-billion-plan

29 An example: Merkus, S., Willems, T., Schipper, D., van Marrewijk, A., Koppejan, J., Veenswijk, M. & Bakker, H. (2016). 'A Storm is Coming? Collective Sensemaking and Ambiguity in an Inter-organizational Team Managing Railway System Disruptions'. Journal of Change Management, pp. 228-248. DOI: 10.1080/14697017.2016.1219380.

30 https://www.volkskrant.nl/columns-opinie/weg-met-het-hokjesdenken-in-de-landbouw~beac9b7f/

31 NBTC Holland Marketing: HollandCity & Amsterdam. Retrieved from www.nbtc.nl/nl/homepage/actueel/dossiers/hollandcity-amsterdam.htm

32 Retrieved from www.shared-space.org

33 Centre of Expertise Shared Space - NHL Stenden University of Applied Sciences, Leeuwarden (2013). De opbrengsten van 15 jaar shared space [The results of 15 years of shared space]. Outcomes of an evaluation of a shared space in Smallingerland.

34 Ministry of Infrastructure and the Environment, Government of the Netherlands. (2018, April 18). Campaign impact study 'Bob 15 jaar [15 years of BOB]'. Retrieved from www.rijksoverheid.nl/documenten/rapporten/2017/04/18/campagne-effectonderzoek-bob-15-jaar

35 Inspiration for policy innovation:
  – OECD (2017), 'Systems Approaches to Public Sector Challenges: Working with Change' Paris: OECD Publishing. Retrieved from dx.doi.org/10.1787/9789264279865-en
  – NESTA. (2011, November). Prototyping Public Services: An introduction to using prototyping in the development of public services. Retrieved from https://media.nesta.org.uk/documents/prototyping_public_services.pdf
  – Lappalainen, P., Markkula, M. & Kune, H. (eds.). (2015). Orchestrating Regional Innovation Ecosystems – Espoo Innovation Garden. Aalto University, Laurea University of Applied Sciences & Built Environment Innovations RYM Ltd. Retrieved from urbanmill.org/2015/04/29/espoo-innovation-garden-book-published-orchestrating-regional-innovation-ecosystems
  – Dutch Ministry of Economic Affairs. (2017). 'Sturen in een verweven dynamiek: Perspectieven op complexiteit en oriëntaties voor beleid [Management in an interwoven dynamic: perspectives on complexity and orientation for policy directions]'. Retrieved from https://edepot.wur.nl/412976

36 Cook, J.W. & Tönurist, P. (2016). 'From Transactional to Strategic: systems approaches to public service challenges', Alpha version, OECD, Observatory of Public Sector Innovation, p.16. Retrieved from www.oecd.org/media/oecdorg/satellitesites/opsi/contents/images/h2020_systemsthinking-fin.pdf

37 Retrieved from https://www.eigen-kracht.nl/what-we-do-family-group-conferencing-participation-selfreliance-citizens/

38 Civic initiative 'Stop de bouw van windmolens op land [Halt the construction of onshore wind turbines]'. Retrieved from stopdebouwvanwindmolensopland.nl

39 Retrieved from mijnkinderarts.nl/baby/vaccinatie/weerstanden-tegen-vaccineren

40 Arlie Russell Hochschild (2016). Strangers in Their Own Land: Anger and Mourning on the American Right. New York: The New Press Publishers; Müller, J-W. (2016). What is Populism? Philadelphia: Penn Press.

41 Cuperus, R. (2014, October 20). 'De Slag om Zwarte Piet is allesbehalve onschuldig [The battle over Zwarte Piet is anything but innocuous]'. De Volkskrant. Retrieved from https://www.volkskrant.nl/nieuws-achtergrond/de-slag-om-zwarte-piet-is-allesbehalve-onschuldig~b2e91d95/

42 Retrieved from https://www.anderetijden.nl/artikel/598/nam-weet-sinds-1963-van-bodemverzakkingen-groningen

43 Retrieved from historiek.net/gaswinning-in-groningen-geschiedenis-gevolgen

44 Retrieved from www.vn.nl/co2-liever-onder-de-grond

45 Retrieved from: https://www.govtech.com/civic/San-Franciscos-Startup-in-Residence-Program-Seeks-to-Expand-Across-North-America.html

46 drift.eur.nl/nl

47 Organizations that focus on promoting societal interests such as the interests of consumers, healthcare, nature and the environment, elder care, development cooperation and so on.